BFI Modern Classics

D0968320

Edward Buscombe and Rob White
Series Editors

Advancing into its second century, the cinema is now a mature art form
with an established list of classics. But contemporary cinema is so
subject to every shift in fashion regarding aesthetics, morals and ideas
that judgments on the true worth of recent films are liable to be risky
and controversial; yet they are essential if we want to know where the
cinema is going and what it can achieve.

As part of the British Film Institute's commitment to the
promotion and evaluation of contemporary cinema, and in conjunction
with the influential BFI Film Classics series, BFI Modern Classics is a
series of books devoted to individual films of recent years. Distinguished
film critics, scholars and novelists explore the production and reception
of their chosen films in the context of an argument about the film's
quality and importance. Insightful, considered, often impassioned, these
elegant, well-illustrated books will set the agenda for debates about what
matters in modern cinema.

Women on the Verge of a Nervous Breakdown

(Mujeres al
borde de un ataque
de nervios)

**Peter
William
Evans**

BRITISH FILM INSTITUTE

bfi

BFI PUBLISHING

First published in 1996 by the
British Film Institute
21 Stephen St, London W1P 2LN

The British Film Institute exists to promote
appreciation, enjoyment, protection and
development of moving image culture in and
throughout the whole of the United Kingdom.
Its activities include the National Film and
Television Archive; the National Film Theatre;
the Museum of the Moving Image;
the London Film Festival; the production and
distribution of film and video; funding and
support for regional activities; Library and
Information Services; Stills, Posters and
Designs; Research, Publishing and Education;
and the monthly *Sight and Sound* magazine.

Designed by Andrew Barron &
Collis Clements Associates

Typeset in Garamond Simoncini
by Fakenham Photosetting Ltd

Printed in Great Britain by Trinity Press,
Worcester

British Library Cataloguing-in-Publication Data
A catalogue record for this book is available
from the British Library
ISBN 0–85170–540–5

Contents

Dedication

For Tom and Jenny

Acknowledgments

I should like to thank Ana Marquesán, the Director of Archives at the Filmoteca in Zaragoza for making all facilities available to me; I was also helped there by David Ruiz and Teresa Serra. Thanks are also due to the staff, especially Marga Lobo and Dolores Devesa, at the Filmoteca in Madrid, where I was able to view various films of crucial interest to this study. For their help, hospitality and friendship I owe an enormous debt of gratitude to all my colleagues in the Department of English and German Studies at the University of Zaragoza, where I spent a wonderful semester on a Fellowship from the Spanish Ministry of Education and Science, a period during which much of this book was researched and written. My special thanks there to Susana Onega, Ignacio Vázquez, José María Bardavío, Chantal Cornut-Gentille, and the person in that department with whom I have collaborated most over the last few years there, Celestino Deleyto, as well as the secretaries Begoña Póveda, Berta Sanz and Cinta Lapuerta. Thanks too to Hilaria Loyo and Constanza del Río who lent me material and discussed film theory and psychoanalysis with me, and to my students at Queen Mary and Westfield College, University of London, for lively discussions on Almodóvar. I am grateful to Agustín Almodóvar and to Paz Sufrategui for making available to me at El Deseo files related to *Mujeres al borde de un ataque de nervios.* I have received much help, encouragement and support from Ed Buscombe and Rob White at the BFI, and from Agustín Sánchez Vidal, Miguel Angel Ramón, Dora Marteles, Carmen Mas, Stephen Roberts, María José Martínez Jurico, Mark Millington, Robin Fiddian, Manucha Lisboa, Nuria Triana Toribio, Bruce Babington, my mother Rose-Marie Evans to whom I owe so much (and here especially her knowledge of French) and, as ever, Isabel.

1 Synopsis

Madrid in the late 80s. Iván (Fernando Guillén) breaks up with his lover
Pepa (Carmen Maura). Both are actors, appearing on TV and dubbing
films. Iván's way of informing Pepa that he is finishing with her is by
leaving a message on the answerphone, asking her to pack his things in
a suitcase. Pepa becomes very agitated – she has also just discovered
that she is pregnant – and decides to put her flat up for sale. Soon
afterwards Iván's son Carlos (Antonio Banderas) and his fiancée Marisa
(Rossy de Palma) visit the flat, with a view to buying it. Carlos sees
his father's photograph in one of the rooms, and both he and Pepa
suddenly become aware of each other's existence. Carlos' mother Lucía
(Julieta Serrano), Iván's mistress in the 60s, now released from a

psychiatric clinic, has recently been living at her parents' home, and is
now in hot pursuit of Pepa whom she suspects of accompanying Iván on
a foreign trip. Pepa has been trying to find Iván (at work and elsewhere)

Marisa's Pepa-induced Midsummer Night's Dream

but unsuccessfully. On some of these journeys she is transported by a sympathetic taxi-driver (Guillermo Montesinos) who seems always to appear conveniently whenever she needs him. Meanwhile, back at the flat, Carlos and Marisa are joined by Candela (María Barranco) who has realised her Middle Eastern lover is a fundamentalist Shiite terrorist planning a bombing outrage in Madrid. She and Carlos ring the police to tip them off anonymously. But the police and a telephone repair man (who has been called in to fix the phone destroyed by Pepa in one of her fits of rage against the unreachable Iván) eventually show up at the flat. There, like Marisa, they fall victim to the drugged gazpacho that has been prepared by Pepa – for herself or for Iván? – and miss out on the chase that takes place when Pepa, transported again by her favourite taxi-driver, and Lucía, who has hijacked a motorcycle and its rider, head for the airport, where Iván is discovered on the point of embarking on a journey with his new girlfriend, the lawyer Paulina (Kitti Manver), to Stockholm. There Iván is saved by Pepa from being killed by Lucía, who is then returned to the hospital. Ivan makes an offer of reconciliation to Pepa, but she declines and returns to her flat, to be reunited with Marisa, who awakens from her slumber. For a moment both women enjoy each other's company in the stillness of a flat at last temporarily released from the spell of sexual desire.

2 Comedy and Melodrama

**I wish to God I could make him cry.
I wish I could make him cry and tread
the floor and feel his heart heavy and
big and festering in him. I wish I could hurt
him like hell.**
        Dorothy Parker, 'A Telephone Call'

Mujeres al borde de un ataque de nervios/Women on the Verge of a Nervous Breakdown (1988) is one of the most commercially successful films ever made in Spain. Shot on a modest budget of £700,000, it went on to gross well over £5,500,000 and in the process won both best script and best actress (Carmen Maura) awards at Venice. *Women on the Verge* made a major international impact after Orion took on its world-wide distribution, and was especially popular in the USA, where speculation arose over the possibility of a re-make with Jane Fonda, Goldie Hawn or Cher.[1] The film's success led in Spain to imitation, with, for instance, *Cómo ser mujer y no morir en el intento / How to Be a Woman and Not Die in the Attempt* (Ana Belén, 1991) which not only starred Carmen Maura but also used promotional posters in the Pop Art graphics style of its forerunner.

The success of *Women on the Verge* can be explained in a number of ways. Marketing and publicity were adeptly handled. A poster for the film's American release, for instance, had Julieta Serrano and Carmen Maura at the centre of the frame; above, the film's topicality and relevance to contemporary US society were highlighted – 'A comedy about someone you know' – while its respectability and box-office success were underlined through approving quotations from prominent US film critics, including Pauline Kael of *The New Yorker,* David Denby of the *New York Magazine* and Steven Schiff of *Vanity Fair*. At the bottom of the frame the director's status as auteur was emphasised with the words, 'A film by Almodóvar'. Indeed, in general, the pressbook projected Almodóvar as a star in his own right, a ploy that recalls that adopted to promote the films of Lubitsch or Hitchcock. More importantly, the film's style and content captivated audiences, who were drawn to its ultra-modernity, its eye for colour – less garish here than in other, more Punk or Euro-Trash Almodóvar films such as *Kika* (1993) – and its capacity for capturing life, as Vicente Molina-Foix puts it, like an instantaneous camera recording topical priorities and obsessions (1993: 21).[2] Above all, though, the film's appeal can be traced to its predominantly comic explorations of subjectivity, sexuality and the relations between the sexes. *Women on the Verge* confirmed Almodóvar's talent for representing complex but plausible female characters – a talent not always appreciated by Spanish film critics who sometimes damn Almodóvar with faint praise, characterising him as a director of brilliance rather than depth (see, for instance, Fernández Santos 1990: 35).

––––––––––

Having worked in theatre, pop music and adult comics, Almodóvar began in films by making Super 8 productions (the first in 1974) with provocative titles such as *Fólleme, fólleme, fólleme, Tim / Fuck Me, Fuck Me, Fuck Me, Tim* (1978). The earliest full-length feature – made largely at Carmen Maura's instigation – was *Pepi, Luci, Bom y otras chicas del montón / Pepi, Luci, Bom, and the Other Girls in the Heap* (1979), a film that immediately associated Almodóvar with the so-called Madrid 'Movida' generation, a sort of Punk-Pop Spanish equivalent of the Bloomsbury set, made up of young artists and radicals who had quickly taken full advantage of the end of *Franquismo*. While a taste for outrage has never really abandoned him – even a film as late as *Kika* still honours the memory of Punk, especially in the characterisation of the scarred, camera-wielding, false-breasts-exposing Reality Show TV hostess played by Victoria Abril – Almodóvar has gradually toned down some of the more gratuitous effects in favour of a more subtle treatment of sexuality and the relations between the sexes. *Laberinto de pasiones /*

Labyrinth of Passions (1982) and *Entre tinieblas / Dark Habits* (1983) reflect this developing maturity, even though they cannot altogether resist adult comic-book style caricature (as when in the former a man habitually sleeps with his daughter because he thinks she is his wife, and in the latter, the source for *Sister Act* (Emile Ardolino, 1992), a woman seeking refuge from gangsters enters a convent where, among other eccentricities, one of the sisters keeps a pet tiger).

The three films leading up to *Women on the Verge – ¿Qué he hecho yo para merecer esto?/What Have I Done to Deserve This?* (1984), *Matador* (1986) and *La ley del deseo / The Law of Desire* (1987) – represent, together with *Women on the Verge*, Almodóvar's most elegant and insightful treatment of the vicissitudes of desire. In the first, the focus is on a woman's struggle for release from the brutalities and frustrations of a loveless marriage; in the second, a narrative about death-obsessed lovers is underpinned by an analysis of the complexities of sexual orientation; in the third, the depiction of the ecstasies and despair of a gay love affair foregrounds the extremes to which lovers will submit in the quest for emotional fulfilment.

In all of these films, as well as in those that follow *Women on the Verge – Atame/Tie Me Up, Tie Me Down* (1989), *Tacones lejanos/High Heels* (1991), *Kika* (1993) and *La flor de mi secreto/The Flower of My Secret* (1995) – both the sights and sounds of Hollywood and the traditions of Spanish cinema are persistently alluded to. Hollywood comedy and melodrama, above all, are recalled, but so are the conventions of the thriller. Almodóvar's films are informed by the popular comedies and melodramas of his national cinema, but sometimes also, perhaps unexpectedly, by the drives and patterns of 'auteurist' traditions (in *What Have I Done to Deserve This?*, for example, the Italian neo-realism of such films as *Muerte de un ciclista / Death of a Cyclist* (Juan Antonio Bardem, 1955) is clearly invoked).

This rich mixture of styles, blending Pop aesthetics with a powerful treatment of sexuality, has meant that in Spain Almodóvar's films have been especially popular with youth and sexually dissident audiences, whose tastes, as Marvin D'Lugo argues (1991: 48), had previously been catered for in such films as Jaime de Armiñán's *Mi querida señorita / My dear Mistress* (1971), Vicente Aranda's *Cambio de sexo / Change of Sex* (1976), Carlos Saura's *Deprisa deprisa / Hurry, Hurry* (1980) and Fernando Trueba's *Opera prima* (1980). These films had gone some way towards creating a favourable climate for the more colourful discussion of sex and gender-related issues in Almodóvar's films. To an extent, his films are the tongue-in-cheek equivalents of the sex manuals and guidebooks that flooded the market after the death of Franco, when the representation and discussion of sexuality were no longer deemed to be taboo.[3]

Under Franco the laws of censorship had been extremely strict (see Gubern 1980, Hopewell 1986, Vincendeau 1995). The censor's office had been set up in 1937, but only after the fall of the Republic in the Civil War were its decrees enforced with ruthless efficiency. In 1939 the public use of Catalan was prohibited, and, in order to establish the hegemony of Castilian at the expense both of regional and other languages, a policy requiring the compulsory dubbing of all foreign films was introduced. As regards the censorship of a film's content, the key player was the Catholic Church which insisted on the upholding of its values in public spectacles, and, as a result, sympathetic treatments of divorce, suicide or extramarital sex were prohibited.[4] Censorship was abolished in 1977, two years after the end of the regime, and although *Women on the Verge* was made eleven years later, its energy still to a certain extent derives, just as much as that of *Pepi, Luci, Bom* (made only two years after the abolition), from the new uninhibited climate.

Leaving aside autobiographical considerations (such as Almodóvar's wish to take a parting shot at his former employers at the national telephone company), the initial inspiration for *Women on the Verge* was a one-act play by Cocteau entitled *La Voix humaine*, and more indirectly, the Spanish stage comedy tradition of dramatists such as Mihura (1905–77) and Jardiel Poncela (1901–52). Filmically, *Women on the Verge* was inspired by the traditions of both Hollywood and Spanish cinema. Its narrative is precariously balanced between melodrama and comedy, and this hybridity typifies Almodóvar's confessed taste for generic confusion (Kinder, 1987: 37). There are traces too, as in other Almodóvar films, of Dorothy Parker's 'Anything Goes' Algonquin Round Table narratives, especially the story entitled 'A Telephone Call', in which the female narrator becomes increasingly frantic as she awaits her lover's promised but never materialising phone-call (Parker, 1989).[5]

Cocteau's play, written in 1930 and performed first by Berthe Bovy and subsequently by Simone Signoret, turns on the narrative of a woman – the only character to appear on stage – abandoned by her lover, whose affections she attempts to revive by declaring her love over the phone. Cocteau's rejected mistress is a *'victime médiocre'* (1983: 16) whose inexhaustible capacity for self-incrimination – *'Oh! mon chéri, ne t'excuse pas, c'est très naturel et c'est moi qui suis stupide'* / 'Oh! My dear don't be sorry, it's very natural, and I'm the stupid one' (23) – brings her not the lover for whom she pines but the spectre of ever more painful memories and desperate thoughts. In its last moments, as the rejected woman repeats the phrase *'je t'aime'* five times (63), the play confirms its fidelity to the conventions of melodrama. *Women on the Verge*, on the other hand, ends with the abandoned woman – no *'victime médiocre'* by any stretch of the imagination – repaying her lover in kind, refusing an offer for reconciliation and, released at least for a time from the slavery of desire, preferring the company of another woman in his place.

Despite the far more positive ending of *Women on the Verge* – at least in its concession to its heroine's momentary triumph over adversity – the film's affiliation to melodrama (both indigenous and American) is never entirely relinquished. As many commentators have noted, the key Hollywood references in the film are to Screwball and 50s comedy – especially *How to Marry a Millionaire* (Jean Negulesco, 1953) – to the musical – especially *The Apartment* (Billy Wilder, 1960) and *Funny Face* (Stanley Donen, 1957) – and to the emotional dramas of Hitchcock, Sirk, Cukor and Ray.[6] In a similar way, as it swings from one mode to another the film is poised between the chic styles designed for the film

by the couturier José María de Cossío and the familiar aesthetics of a
women's magazine – between stylistic distinctiveness and more
conventional modes of representation. Leaving the discussion of other
allusions for later, I shall concentrate for the moment on references to
Hitchcock and Sirk in a key scene which exemplifies Almodóvar's
characteristically cross-generic style.[7]

There are at least three direct allusions to Hitchcock in the film, all
ultimately related to a shared interest in male anxieties about powerful
women, and especially powerful mothers. The scene in which Lucía
pursues Iván at the airport carries overtones, notably in its use of music,
of *Psycho* (1960); while Pepa's fainting fit at the dubbing studio, where
we see her at one point through the lenses of her fallen spectacles,
recalls a shot from the fairground sequence in *Strangers on a Train* (1953)
where we see, also through the lenses of her pair of spectacles on the
ground, a man strangling a woman. But perhaps the most complex
allusion to Hitchcock occurs between these two moments: having heard
Iván's unwelcome message on the answerphone, Pepa sets out to find
him, in order to confront him in person, and to prevent him perhaps
from wriggling free of his responsibilities as the father of her unborn
child. Thinking he may be at Lucía's flat, she sits outside the building,
staring at it and at neighbouring flats, considering her next move.

As she waits, her gaze wanders from one part of the building in
front of her to another. At one point the camera focuses on a female
dancer – stripped to her underwear – doing some physical exercises, and
then on a man weeping on a balcony, before eventually fixing on a
heated exchange between Lucía and Carlos, Lucía's son by Iván. This is
a moment, according to Celestino Deleyto, where Pepa 'gradually learns
to look at the world from the outside, and becomes increasingly
interested in the story of Iván as a narrative, arguably transferring her
sexual desire for him to a desire for narrative' (1995: 54).

Deleyto's observation belongs to an extended discussion of *Women
on the Verge* as a post-modernist film in which self-referentiality, parody
and cool detachment all compromise the text's capacity for faithful

reflection of observable reality. Nothing is seen directly: subjectivity is mediated through the imagery of popular culture, or otherwise seen to be distorted or fractured (as when the faces of the characters are reflected in the broken glass or front-door peep-hole at Pepa's flat). The ubiquitous Mambo taxi-driver sums up the post-modernist mood when he is delighted to be ordered by Pepa to follow the car in front because he had believed that sort of thing only happened in films. Even though this film opened up an international audience for Almodóvar's work beyond the ghetto of post-modernism and Punk comedy, Deleyto is right to stress the film's elaborate artifice: for, as Almodóvar has himself pointed out, the stylisation and cross-generic contextualisation of emotional drama are fundamental aspects of his technique:

On occasion, High Comedy includes elements from terror, or adventure movies. For example, a million things happen all at once and the lives of the leading characters are usually hanging by a thread. But instead of having jungles, Indians, waterfalls, evil ones possessed by the devil, living corpses or hidden treasure, the action takes place in the heart of the middle-class family (the kitchen, living-room, bedroom etc.), or a bar in some lounge or cafe, or in a museum or an art auction. The tension is never produced by blood, and the characters, although they hate each other, hardly ever commit murder, even though they act as if they're capable of doing so.
(Almodóvar, 1988: 10)

A characteristic feature of 'post-modernist' films is a self-conscious pattern of allusions to other films. Almodóvar relies on the viewer's ability to recognise references, drawing him/her into a sort of pleasurable film quiz as the film rolls along. At more profound levels, though, the film's collage of quotations reinforces Almodóvar's post-modernist theme about the provisional and artificial nature of meaning; furthermore, it celebrates the radical potential of popular culture in a country where for nearly forty years popular film was identified with ideological banalities, and where the only complexity was to be found in the more sober, 'auteurist' films, targeted at minority audiences, by such directors as Carlos Saura and Victor Erice.

The Hitchcock reference here noted by Deleyto – to *Rear Window* (1954) – encompasses both suspense (in the sense defined by Almodóvar) and melodrama. In *Rear Window,* the James Stewart character, immobilised by a broken leg, spends much of his time looking through his powerful telephoto lens out of his flat window at events taking place in the building opposite. He sees, among other things (most dramatically, the aftermath of a man's murder of his wife), a scantily clad female dancer, exercising to music. The woman spied on by Pepa in the scene outside Lucía's house strongly recalls Hitchcock's scenario. *Rear Window*'s protagonist (James Stewart) is portrayed not just as an

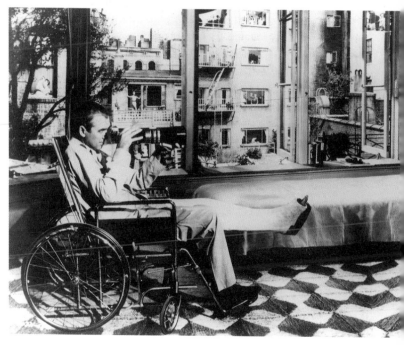

Pepa's voyeuristic precursor, L. B. Jeffries (James Stewart) in *Rear Window* (Hitchcock, 1954)

imperilled newspaper photographer in danger of attack by a wife-murderer (Raymond Burr), but also as an outsider, an oedipally traumatised male voyeur who is content to live vicariously through detached involvement in the affairs of others, horrified by the thought of commitment, especially to assertive women of the kind played by Grace Kelly. The significance of Almodóvar's reference to Hitchcock's study of voyeurism lies in its prompting of the audience's stock of film memories so that the scene's post-modernist insecurities are underlined (as if to insist that the film is merely reflecting another film, not reality) at the same time as questions about commitment and personal relationships are raised.

The key difference with *Rear Window* is that the voyeur in Almodóvar's film is female. Pepa's intertextual identification with James Stewart's L. B. Jeffries reverses the process of voyeuristic or fetishistic pleasure through her appropriation of the gaze. In a shot that is also traced over with various recollections of the visual rhetoric of one of Hollywood's greatest melodramatists, Douglas Sirk, Almodóvar makes Pepa observe the distant nocturnal scene of quarrelling mother and son through a carefully constructed image where, at the left of the frame, tree leaves – as if hinting here at impermanence – and, at its base, house railings – as if suggesting the rigidities of the social order – provide the dominant perspectives through which the relationship between the couple is glimpsed. In this act of ordered looking, Pepa becomes aware of the suffocations of family life caused by the torments of passion. Separating the troubled characters in the frame within the frame, right in the middle, is a suitcase placed on a table, an object uninteresting in itself but whose pillar-box red colour – one of the film's many reds, given prominence here through the glare of the room's artificial light – offers a focus for reflection on the origins and evanescence of desire.

Sirk's *mise en scène*, as Thomas Elsaesser (1987) and others have argued, carries in its aesthetics of excess an indirect critique of the predominantly conservative society in which his 40s and 50s films were made.[8] If dialogue – whenever innocent of irony – is often obliged to register quite banal ideological orthodoxies, *mise en scène*, like music, can often be relied on to set a tone of dissidence. When Fassbinder (1972) remarked that Sirk's films taught him to love excess, he was only partially motivated by a characteristically irreverent wish to denounce the bourgeois aesthetics of decorum. More profoundly, this defence of the transgressive aesthetics of bad taste reveals a sense, shared also by Almodóvar, of how orthodoxy can be exposed subtly, if paradoxically, in excessive cinematic gestures. The major difference, though, between Almodóvar (and, for that matter, Fassbinder) and Sirk lies in the conditions of production prevalent during their respective careers. In Hollywood during the 40s and 50s there were severe constraints on the explicit treatment of particular topics; in post-censorship Spain during the 80s and 90s such constraints did not, and do not, apply. Almodóvar has never had to practice circumspection in the manner of Sirk.

Almodóvar's admiration of Sirk and his respect for melodrama's free expression of sentiment, extreme situations, colour and intensity often leads to a pronounced element of kitsch, a mode with which he clearly enjoys a love-hate relationship, in his films.[9] The homage to Sirk is wittily announced in the title of a piece which Almodóvar included in a collection of his writings, *Patty Diphusa y otros textos / Patty Diphusa and Other Texts* (1991). The piece in question, 'Escrito sobre el escroto' / 'Written on the Scrotum' punningly alludes to Sirk's *Written on the Wind* (1956), since in Spanish only one letter distinguishes between 'written' (*escrito*) and 'scrotum' (*escroto*). More significantly, Sirkian thematics are clearly reflected, for instance, in *What Have I Done to Deserve This?* and *The Flower of My Secret*, the Almodóvar equivalents of the woman-centred melodrama to which Sirk was drawn and of which notable examples are *Magnificent Obsession* (1953), *All That Heaven Allows* (1954) and *Imitation of Life* (1958). In *What Have I Done to Deserve This?* Gloria (Carmen Maura), trapped in a dismal marriage to a brutal husband (Angel de Andrés López), strives to overcome the hardships of a miserable life in the poorer suburbs of Madrid; in *The Flower of My Secret*, Leo (Marisa Paredes) discover, like Lori (Lana

Turner) in *Imitation of Life,* that professional success (in this case as a writer of romantic novels) amounts to very little when her love life is in ruins. The formal qualities of Almodóvar's more mature films – above all in their use of framing, colour and music – are also distinctively reminiscent of Sirkian practice.

Concentrating for the moment on colour, one notices how blues and reds are used to stunning effect in *All That Heaven Allows* to create contrasts of feeling: when Carrie (Jane Wyman) prepares to break out of her mummified existence as a sexless widow, she puts on a low-cut, pillar-box-red evening dress. The passionate intent registered by her choice of dramatic colour is at odds with her children's sense of decorum: their disapproval finds its visual equivalent in the film's use of cool blue lighting for the background decor. In *Women on the Verge* there

Sirk's inspirational mise en scène from *All that Heaven Allows* (1954)

is a similar alignment of emotional meaning and visual effect. In an early scene, for example, when Iván begins to leave a message for Pepa on the answerphone his superficially affectionate words are given an ironic visual commentary through the lurid blue perspex shield of the phone booth from which he is dialling: 'Pepa? Pepa? Darling. Are you asleep? As I'm in a hurry, we've started without you.' The shot drains Iván of his natural facial colour while imposing upon him a blueness consistently identified with coolness and distance. A contrast is immediately established in the next scene where we see Pepa dash, too late, to reach the phone. She wears fuchsia-coloured pyjamas, one of many reds she will wear in the film as an index of her passionate feelings. To make the contrast even clearer, Almodóvar has Pepa later on use the same telephone booth at the dubbing studio, only this time the shot is taken

Iván (Fernando Guillén), the prisoner of desire

not through the blue perspex, but through the gap, allowing the character's natural colours to be unaffected by artifical hues.

As María Antonia García de León and Teresa Maldonado remark (1989), this Sirkian aesthetic, moreover, bequeathed Almodóvar a set of instruments through which to intensify the colour and visual flair of the Spanish cinema, creating a distance between the boldly colourful look of all his films and the more austere tones of auteurist ones (by Saura, Erice, Borau and others), which reflected the gloom of the Franco years. At times the film seems, as many have noted – for instance Hansen (1988: 88) and Walters (1989: 3) – more preoccupied with big hair, eye-liners, haute couture and fashion accessories than with the vicissitudes of desire.[10] But popular, box-office-determined Spanish comedies had already anticipated the production values of films like *Pepi, Luci, Bom*, *Labyrinth of Passions* and *Women on the Verge*. In the 50s and 60s comedies of such enormously popular directors as Mariano Ozores and Pedro Lazaga and also in such films as *Las chicas de la cruz roja / The Red Cross Girls* (Rafael Salvia, 1958), *Los tramposos / The Tricksters* (Pedro Lazaga, 1959), *Objetivo Bikini / Bikini Mission* (Mariano Ozores, 1968), the decor, fashions, pastel colours and cosmetics, are all used straight, in what are really soft-porn narratives mediating the sexual repression of the times; in Almodóvar's films there is always a tension between straightness and campy, knowing parody.

As Pepa observes the multiple scenes unfolding before her outside Lucía's house, her view – and ours – is filtered through this double-focused lens of Hollywood melodrama (as exemplified by both Hitchcock and Sirk) and Spanish comedy. And as she looks, so she too is in turn observed by Marisa (Rossy de Palma), whose eyes stare out from their reflection in the car mirror while she waits outside the building where her lover Carlos is attempting to cope with the hysteria of his demented mother. In becoming the object of another's gaze, Pepa's perspective itself becomes relativised, in the process emphasising once again the film's infection by various genres and film traditions, melodrama crossed with comedy. Like Chus Lampreave, Julieta Serrano and Kitti Manver, Rossy de Palma is one of Almodóvar's regulars, still there in *The Flower of My Secret* as a sort of Ugly Sister whose more mundane preoccupations place in critical perspective the flights of fancy of more glamorous lovers. She is the comically grotesque equivalent of all those second-string actors like Ralph Bellamy or Thelma Ritter who were never romantic enough to get Katharine Hepburn or Rock

Hudson, having to make do with lesser lights, forming couples who drew attention to the norms rather than to the ideals of love. Her exotic bird features, especially her toucan beak, belong to comedy's traditional disrespect for the body: Falstaff's belly, Barbara Windsor's breasts, Jimmy Durante's nose, or even Arnold Schwarzenegger's biceps – in *Twins* (Ivan Reitman, 1988) at least – are familiar targets of ridicule, collapsing divisions of gender, class, race and nationality (Brunovska and Jenkins, 1995: 1–13). At first the joke is on her: appearing initially as a stultified, implausibly self-assured harridan who dominates her fiancé Carlos, she is transformed at the end of the film in the dream ambience of Pepa's flat, her virginal inviolability giving way after an erotic dream induced by the spiked gazpacho to a less priggish demeanour and attitude and to the belief that she has magically lost her virginity. In this and in many other films in which she appears (*Tie Me Up, Tie Me Down* and *The Flower of My Secret,* for example), Rossy de Palma's face forces comedy into melodrama, providing a silent comic commentary on scenes threatening to topple over into melodramatic anguish and hysteria.

To the principals involved in crises of desire the pain of love is all too real; to those spared the torments of ill-matched passions, the sight of warring lovers can seem merely ridiculous. The relations between melodrama and romantic comedy – genres which have predominantly female perspectives – have been thoughtfully summarised by Kathleen Rowe: 'Whereas melodrama allows the transgressive woman to triumph only in her suffering, romantic comedy takes her story to a different end, providing a sympathetic place for female resistance to masculine authority and an alternative to the suffering femininity affirmed by melodrama' (1995: 41–2). Almodóvar has drawn attention both to *Women on the Verge*'s allegiance to these generic formats and to its reworking of genres:

In *Women on the Verge* ... I sometimes respect the rule of comedy and at times I don't respect it at all. The format, decor, dramatic organisation belong to comedy, as does the performance of the

actors who speak quickly, as if they weren't thinking about what they were saying. But at times the narrative is not specific to comedy. In comedy one would almost never find, for instance, a close-up of a microphone like the one I used in the dubbing sequence. Comedy uses medium shots basically. The organisation of the film also fails to respect the norms of comedy, probably because of this indiscipline I have towards genres and also because I wanted to stress other dramatic elements.

(Strauss, 1995: 93–4)

The partially comic structure of *Women on the Verge* follows this pattern. It focuses on the lives of a number of women most of whom have in some ways been pushed towards nervous breakdown through disastrous relations with men, in a narrative that hinges, as in much romantic comedy, on the exposure of the conformist male's limitations. Whereas in classical Hollywood romantic comedy – above all in Screwball[11] – the finale usually finds the male not only exposed and humiliated but also eventually rehabilitated – as, for instance, in *Bringing up Baby* (Howard Hawks, 1938) or *The Lady Eve* (Preston Sturges, 1941) – *Women on the Verge* leaves Iván to confront his own wearisome limitations in solitude. The comedy of Iván's situation lies in the disparity between the ambitions of his narcissistic self-image and the reality of his failure as lover, father and man.

———

Many contemporary comedies, both in Spain and in Hollywood, surround their closures with ambiguity: in Woody Allen's films, above all, but also in other American films, such as *Sleepless in Seattle* (Nora Ephron, 1993*), Something Wild* (Jonathan Demme, 1986), *Peggy Sue Got Married* (Francis Ford Coppola, 1986) and *French Kiss* (Lawrence Kasdan, 1995), and, in Spain, *Amo tu cama rica / I Love Your Nice Bed* (Emilio Martínez Lázaro, 1993), *Todos los hombres sois iguales / You Men*

The prefiguration of the Madonna and Child motif from *Matador* (1986)

Are All Alike (Manuel Gómez Pereira, 1994) or *Boca a boca / Mouth to Mouth* (Manuel Gómez Pereira, 1995), the endings are provisional, leaving the audience ultimately uncertain, despite the union of the romantic couple, of that union's durability. These films try to reconcile, sometimes awkwardly, the offscreen reality of divorce, single-parenting, failed relationships and fears of commitment with an ideal of stability in heterosexual relationships. In Spain the treatment of romantic love is given even sharper focus in the context of changes taking place (such as greater permissiveness, cohabitation, divorce, abortion reform) in the country since the death of Franco, though it must also be acknowledged that Franco was not the inventor of conservative morality in Spain, merely perhaps its most efficient purveyor.

In its frustration of the couple's reconciliation, *Women on the Verge* seems even more radical at its closure when it veers increasingly towards melodrama. Iván's punishment is approved in a kind of displaced discrediting of the *ancien régime* whose representative he is. Whereas Alfredo Landa, José Luis López Vázquez, Fernando Esteso, Andrés Pajares, Tony Leblanc and other male stars of 60s and 70s Spanish comedies may not have been expected to problematise their masculinity or to interrogate stock attitudes towards women, the same could not be said of a late 80s modern male, whose self-scrutiny can be taken to the extremes of the Antonio Bandaras character in *Matador,* whose sense of guilt is so advanced that he confesses to murders of which he is innocent.

3 Men and Women

I suppose a man could do over his office, but he never thinks of anything so simple. No dear, a man has only one escape from his old self – to see a different self in the mirror of some woman's eyes
The Women (George Cukor, 1939)

As soon as Pepa hears Iván's recorded message about his wish to dissolve their affair, her flat becomes the space where at some point almost all the characters will converge, the space set aside for metamorphosis. Although in its stress on renewal the comedy of *Women on the Verge* reproduces some of the patterns of classical narratives, the transformations are almost exclusively those of the female characters, while the males, especially Iván, are punished, either explicitly or implicitly, for their embodiment of the supremacist values identified with the discredited pre-1975 political order. Pepa's flat, already prepared with its array of wildfowl for service as the archetypal magical 'green world' of comedy where renewals occur, becomes a space purged of patriarchal dominance, hospitable to ideological reconstruction. When Candela arrives she remarks: *'Esto parece cosa de terrorismo'*/'This looks like something done by a terrorist.' The exclamation is ambiguous: terrified by the implications of her association with Shiite terrorists, she compares the setting – with its smashed telephone and windows, and charred double-bed – to a bomb site; knowing what Pepa has been through with her own terrorist, Iván, we note the relevance of her remark to what was once the site of desire, a space that requires reconstruction before Pepa can reclaim her self-respect.

The symbolic despatch through the penthouse window of Iván's suitcase and the ritual incendiary of the lovers' bed are the preliminary steps towards making the flat a place fit for more innocent creatures of nature – the menagerie of birds and men-free women who begin increasingly to occupy the space. Taking its cue in this respect from George Cukor's *The Women*, *Women on the Verge* concentrates on female characters who characteristically display initiative, strength and solidarity in the face of male betrayals in love. In *The Women* neither the viewers nor the deceived wife ever set eyes on the Norma Shearer character's errant husband. The pattern is to a large extent retained in *Women on the Verge* where right until the end Pepa, too, is denied a glimpse of her treacherous lover. As also in Jean Negulesco's *How to Marry a Millionaire*, the flat acquires a symbolic centrality, but whereas the women in the Negulesco film periodically denude it of furniture in order to fund their strategy for landing eligible wealthy bridegrooms, Pepa's expulsions of household items signify cathartic release from perfidious men. The one exception to this rule of a male-free zone (if one discounts the temporary and official presence of the telephone repair man and the police hunting the caller who tipped them off about

Norma Shearer, Joan Crawford and Rosalind Russell, George Cukor's women in *The Women* (1939)

the Shiite gang) is Carlos, the benighted, initially somewhat insipid son of Iván and Lucía.

Despite Carlos's infiltration of the sanctuary, the flat becomes progressively more female-dominated as Candela, Marisa and Lucía all gravitate towards its charmed ambience. The coda sees Marisa and Pepa draw close to each other, both temporarily absolved from the laws of sexual desire and the society of treacherous men. In a fantasy space within a fantasy city the two women fleetingly share an ideal moment. The city now seems all the more fantastic and magical; it has at some level mutated from a place governed by patriarchal orthodoxies to one ruled by alternative measures, susceptible to infinite transformations. Hailing from a remote vilage in La Mancha, Almodóvar thought of Madrid as a fantasy land; it was here that he first came into contact with Pop, and where he dreamt of Galerías Preciados (a sort of Selfridges) as another person might have dreamt of the Prado or the Louvre:

Cities have slums and pollution, noise and poverty, but their greatness also sometimes lies in these imperfections. ... [Madrid was] a crazy city which amused itself secretly under the dictatorship preparing itself to change vertiginously as soon as the nightmare disappeared. I grew up, enjoyed, suffered, grew fat and developed in Madrid ... my life and my films are tied to Madrid like the two sides of a coin.
(Almodóvar, 1991: 106–7; 108–9)

As Marvin D'Lugo argues, in its representation of the modernity of Spain, the city has become 'an assertion of a vibrant Spanish cultural identity ... built around a rejection of the traditions that ordered Spanish social life for four decades' (1991: 47). These traditions were reflected in Franquist-inspired films that denigrated urban culture while celebrating a folkloric, sanitised Spain, innocent of sexuality, communism and foreign influence.[12] Almodóvar's films are all city-centred. His flight from his own rural origins in Calzada de Calatrava, where he described his presence there as resembling that of an astronaut at the court of King Arthur (Kinder, 1987: 36), seemed to him to be as necessary and dramatic as that of his great precursor, Don Quixote, also of La Mancha. Almodóvar himself draws attention to the ambivalent significance the place occupies in his life: 'Everything I do is in opposition to the education I received in La Mancha, and yet I belong there, with all that that signifies' (Torres, 1995: 39).

In common with the lovers in *A Midsummer Night's Dream*, to which in its use of setting and the magical drugged gazpacho the film refers, or in more immediate film terms, like those in *A Midsummer Night's Sex Comedy* (Woody Allen, 1982) – a comparison made by Almodóvar himself (Strauss, 1995: 102) – or *Smiles of a Summer Night* (Ingmar Bergman, 1955), the characters are momentarily transformed. Like the heroine in the *Sleeping Beauty* fairy-tale, they are eventually roused in this oneiric interior from their psychological and ideological slumber. Their secret place, set apart from the hurly-burly of the metropolis, is magically transformed into a temporary refuge from the harassments of patriarchy. Unlike the claustrophobic flats in Almodóvar's own *What Have I Done to Deserve This?* and Regueiro's brilliant satire of modern married life, *Duerme, duerme mi amor / Sleep, Sleep My Love* (1974), to which *Women on the Verge* and other Almodóvar films are much indebted, Pepa's place undergoes a temporary metamorphosis. In both *Sleep, Sleep My Love* and *What Have I Done to Deserve This?*, the flats remain places of inescapable entrapment. In each case a victimised character fails to find true liberation because of insurmountable social circumstances. In *Women on the Verge* Pepa's situation is ultimately recoverable through inner resources developed in relatively easy social conditions: she has a career, earns a comfortable living, wears designer clothes, enjoys the expensive pleasures of city life and lives in a stylish flat in one of the smartest parts of town. The setting becomes a place of stillness, liberated from the time-obsessed hectic pace – so characteristic of Screwball or high comedy – of contemporary life, while not of course becoming time-locked and spellbound, as with the 60s world of Lucía. The clocks given close-up prominence in early scenes at the dubbing studio and Pepa's flat acquire ironic significance: Pepa eventually moves from one time zone – her regressive relationship with Iván –to another, timeless, dimension, finding temporary release from sexual desire and alternative modes of fulfilment through self-control and inner tranquility.

And yet, of course, as Rossy de Palma's representation of the spirit of comedy in this final scene reminds us, we know that calm will inevitably precede storm, that these revitalised characters will eventually return to the 'civilised' world. The place of comic reversals and truthful revelations in any case remains spatially attached – as in a Chinese box structure – to other perhaps less liberated spaces, such as the flats that belong to the young biker-girl and her lover, and the Jehovah's Witness

concierge, Chus. These are characters who at some levels, and judged by Franquist standards, seem transgressive in their preference for rock and roll or fundamentalist Christianity over more mainstream tastes in music or religion, but who at other levels remain flawed and compromised, the former too seduced by material opportunism, the latter by newer forms

María Barranco, Rossy de Palma, Julieta Serrano and Carmen Maura of authority. Their meanings play into the significance of the building's *mise en scène*, modifying and offering a perspective on Pepa's life. Her penthouse is an exteriorisation of her pent-up feelings, once chaotic, betrayed and even suicidal (a suitable place therefore from which the Shiite-traumatised Candela can attempt to leap to her death). Its Olympian altitude not only gestures towards her high-aiming professional and personal ambitions but also confirms the towering heights from which her hopes of enduring romantic love will eventually tumble.

With Iván's belongings unceremoniously ejected, Pepa's flat begins to assume more personal, less couple-centred significance, and though love has vanished, alternative modes of fulfilment such as independence and solidarity with other women begin to seem like viable alternatives.

In this comic closure, then, the renewal associated with the fortunes and relations of the romantic couple is reformulated as a revitalised process affecting other aspects of a woman's life, an event commemorated at the

The mother-to-be Pepa, brandishing spiked gazpacho, is more potent than Carlos' pistol-packin' real Mama, Lucía (Julieta Serrano)

end by the mutual support represented by the emotional bonding of the mother-to-be Pepa and the no longer virginal Marisa.

————

It is the film's stress on women as mothers – sometimes in problematic images, as when, even though in comic form, Pepa appears in a TV advert as a mother whose psychopathic son eternally eludes the police because his blood-soaked shirts are significantly washed by her in whiter-than-white, not Omo, but Ecce Homo – which opens up the complexities of Iván's subjectivity, an enigma as much to Iván himself as to the women whose lives he has helped throw into turmoil. Although the film is given a predominantly female perspective, the enigma of men, and not women, is – as Pepa puts it to Ana, the biker-girl, in the final chase sequence to the airport – more complex than the machinery of a motorcycle. The tables are turned on Freud: men, rather than women, are reckoned to be the true conundrum of life. Through Iván, Almodóvar focuses on the origins and behavioural patterns of the classic Don Juan, still a revered figure in the more conformist corners of the contemporary Spanish unconscious. Our first glimpse of Iván is in Pepa's dream, where he is seen in a sort of Felliniesque black-and-white 60s film, moving along a line of beautiful women, making admiring comments to each of them, but mockingly, meaninglessly using borrowed words, spoken into a hand-held microphone. As he walks past, he is framed against an architectural background that is unmistakably Moorish, an identification between character and *mise en scène* that immediately links his attitudes with the traditions of that culture.

For Karen Horney, women's attraction to the womaniser may be explained as an 'overvaluation of love' that originates in childhood rejection and leads to a relentless desire to prove 'desirability to an endless number of men, a situation more possible if the objects of desire are Don Juans, by definition not satisfied with one woman' (1967: 208). Fernando Guillén's leading-man roles in the Spanish cinema qualify him

well for the part of a man exercising power over a wide variety of
women: a woman of leisure (Lucía), a colleague at work (Pepa) and a
feminist lawyer (Paulina). This Don Juan – and he went on to play the
real thing in *Don Juan en los infiernos / Don Juan in Hell* (Gonzalo
Suárez, 1992) – even lacks the appeal of youth or beauty of the kind
that, say, Antonio Banderas might have brought to the role.[13] But
Guillén's atraction, like that of Gary Cooper for the Mercedes
Sampietro character in *Gary Cooper que estás en los cielos / Gary Cooper
Who Art in Heaven* (Pilar Miró, 1980), is precisely his middle age and
aura of conformism. The suggestion is that conventional masculinity has
failed to lose its seductiveness over women too oedipalised to notice the
reality of the unreconstructed male, too trusting in an ideology of
romantic love, or else too wary of its wilder, more unpredictable, even
though perhaps more egalitarian, modern forms. The film allows room
for speculation on all these possibilities. Iván is not only Sterling Hayden
– the lover who lives to regret his betrayal – to Pepa's Joan Crawford; he
is also the film's Man in the Grey Flannel Suit, his conformism, though,
inspired not so much by corporate loyalty as by the shared hollowness
and image-obsessed banalities of the consumerist ethos. Like the Bishop
in the dream-within-a-dream sequence of Buñuel's *Le Charme discret de
la bourgeoisie / The Discreet Charm of the Bourgeoisie* (1972), he is
content to speak lines given to him by others, both in his profession as a
dubber of foreign-language films and in his private life where, as if
through osmosis, his subjectivity seems no more substantial than the play
of colour and light on the screen in the dubbing-room, a point brilliantly
made by Almodóvar as he pans, following the light pouring out of its
lens, from the projector to the screen on which flicker the images of
Nicholas Ray's great film *Johnny Guitar* (1954).[14]

The shallowness of the Don Juan figure, here reincarnated as Iván
the Terrible – as Jill Forbes allusively christens him (1989: 135) – may
largely be understood through Melanie Klein's analysis of oedipal desires
which lead in adult life to the simultaneous embracing and desertion of
women who play the role of mother-surrogates from whom the male

paradoxically craves both intimacy and independence (1964: 86). Klein distinguishes between these conflicting drives, stressing the effects of separation of the child at birth from its mother as the cause of human anxiety. On the one hand, the child feels the need to make reparation to the mother (and all achievements in life will be partially motivated by this desire); on the other, all kinds of strategies are mobilised as defences against separation anxiety, including its forceful denial and the refusal to acknowledge the separateness of others, processes set up as if to promote complete self-sufficiency. Comic narratives often split this process through the use of twinned characters, one representing self-sufficiency, the other self-deficiency: Don Quixote and Sancho Panza, Laurel and Hardy, Bob Hope and Bing Crosby, Dean Martin and Jerry Lewis, and so on. More recently, *Twins* has Julius (Arnold Schwarzeneger) embark on a journey to find and reclaim his mother, while his totally unidentical twin brother Vincent (Danny de Vito) represents an ultimately unsuccessful refusal of otherness and a determination, through an attempt to foil Julius's plan, to maintain his inviolability and separateness.

Women on the Verge dramatises this conflict within the same character, now driving Iván towards one woman, now forcing him to abandon her for another. Nowhere treated approvingly, Iván nevertheless partially represents the film's comprehending analysis of an individual's loss of control through conflicting desires. Even at the end of the film, he is still the plaything of these unresolved dualities of feeling. On the point of boarding a plane for Stockholm, he looks with an affectionate eye towards Lucía, even though she has just attempted to shoot him, and then pleads with Pepa, his rescuer from Lucía's aim, to consider resuming their relationship. Iván's representation of the confusions of masculinity is given momentary plausibility, even sympathy, at the precise moment he utters the familar rhetoric of betrayal:

Pepa, I haven't been able to collect the suitcase. I would have liked to talk with you, but I now see you don't want to. In a few days I'll try

again, when you're calmer. I want you to know that the years we have spent together have been the best years of my life. And that I'm not going on a trip with any woman. Goodbye my love. I wish you all the best, from the bottom of my heart.

These are partly the desperate self-absolving gestures of a man whom the audience has already learned to treat as a congenital liar and coward; but they are also characteristic of a lover who has failed to reconcile what Freud (1981) referred to as the often discordant impulses of affection and sensuality. Ivan's unexpectedly moving words indicate the multifariousness of desire. The depth of feeling conveyed in them carries just enough ambiguity for the audience – whatever Pepa says about recognising through the tone of his voice their cynical meaninglessness – to infer that Iván's extreme disorientation prevents him from separating lies from truth.

What is unambiguous here is Almodóvar's conviction that endings and beginnings in love are rarely clean or clear-cut, with regrets and anxieties overlapping from one relationship into another. Like chain-smokers unable to break the habit, lovers often fail to extinguish one passion before lighting up again. As Iván formulates his remarks, the audience cannot avoid feeling torn between revulsion for what may be the glib rhetoric of a practised deceiver (a calling honed to perfection through his career as dubbing actor) and poignant sympathy for his situation, caught as he is in the crossfire of affection and desire. Moreover, although Iván's seduction of women comes across as the attempted resolution of his own narcissistic failures, his confusion may also be readable to a certain extent as both oedipally motivated and, in its transgressive aspects, determined by an unconscious desire to undermine a social system that has taken men as well as women to the verge of nervous breakdown.

In this respect his plight is ultimately no different from Lucía's, since both are in the end the victims of an ideology that prioritises the role of the patriarch while demonising the mother through her compensatory pseudo-empowerment in the home – a theme rightly seen by Marsha Kinder (1993) as representing a significant trend in recent Spanish cinema. The male's quest for the mother, here represented by Iván's childlike gravitation towards assertive disciplinarians (Lucía, Pepa and Paulina), unconsciously registers his flight from the Law of the Father and – though his indoctrination by patriarchal norms of masculinity have hardly prepared him for it – towards an embrace of the feminine, while simultaneously turning him against it. The film thus performs a difficult balancing act. On the one hand, it paints a picture of masculinity in denial, constantly portraying Iván as someone falsely accusing Pepa of avoiding contact with him, refusing to acknowledge the expiry of his own feelings for her as he strives to transfer his own guilt on to her (a strategy which in its repudiation by Pepa further stresses the film's radical sexual politics). On the other hand, in its more

Strindbergian moments, it also falls into line with other texts (by, for instance, St John of the Cross, or even Tirso de Molina, two of Spain's greatest Golden Age writers) that dramatise the dilemmas of men in flight from powerful women.

In Antonio Banderas' role here as Carlos the film sees an

Carlos (Antonio Banderas), the only male welcome in a female sanctuary, flanked by Lucía and Candela (María Barranco)

opportunity to dramatise the male's attempts to seek both exile from the realm of patriarchal authority and refuge in a largely female-dominated terrain, here ruled by Pepa. Banderas is here far more subdued than in the earlier *Law of Desire* or the later *Tie Me Up, Tie Me Down*, where he plays wild, id-driven obsessives. In *Women on the Verge* Banderas' softer side is given greater prominence: Carlos is portrayed as the confused offspring of lunatic parents.

This 'chico Almodóvar' ('Almodóvar boy') was discovered by the director while taking part in 1981 in a stage play by Calderón, one of Spain's greatest classical dramatists. 'You have a very romantic face. Your face would be fantastic for the cinema', Almodóvar is reputed to have told Banderas (Fernández y Oliva, 1995: 89). That judgement, echoed by a remark in *USA Today* – 'his body language is as soft and sweet as a

Guillermo Montesinos' campy cabbie

cha-cha-cha' (quoted in Castellano, 1995: 15) – has led to a variety of
parts and a seemingly infinite series of inflections: the sizzling-hot Latin
Lover New Valentino male sex symbol of such 90s films as *The Mambo
Kings* (Arne Glimcher, 1992), *House of Spirits* (Bille August, 1993) and
Two Much (Fernando Trueba, 1995); the macho action hero of *Assassins*,
the *homme fatale* of *The Law of Desire*; and, to use Banderas' own
description, the somewhat timid ingenu of *Women on the Verge*
(Fernández and Oliva, 1995: 123). Even here, though, Banderas'
latent virility is distinguished from the more deliberately cultivated
androgynous look of Miguel Bosé, the extremely popular epicene
heart-throb singer/actor who appeared in *High Heels* (1991).

In *Women on the Verge*, the permitted access of Banderas as Carlos
to what becomes a sort of female sanctuary is ambivalent: on the one
hand it acknowledges his victimisation and sees in him potential for a
more gentle form of masculinity; on the other it draws attention to the
survival of old habits, since the women here may not ultimately want to
be eternally separated from men, and Carlos is already showing signs of
following in his father's footsteps by wooing Candela as soon as the
drugged gazpacho sends his fiancée Marisa to sleep. Nevertheless,
whatever his ultimate failures and obscure motivations, Carlos
represents – gropingly, perhaps unconsciously – the film's desire to
reverse the legacy of a culture that exalts the male at the expense of the
female, seeing in the latter merely a source of perversity and hysteria.
If Lucía is the film's demonised, patriarchalised nervous wreck from
whom Carlos seeks release, Pepa represents the possibility of a return
to a maternal principle all but lost in the culture's processes of oedipal
normalisation. While one side of Carlos remains under the control of the
Law of the Father, another hungers for identification with what the film
sees as the maternal feminine and its bold, invigorating personification
in Pepa. At one level, then, as he stumbles on to the reality of his
father's relationship with Pepa – when he goes flat hunting with Marisa
– his journey takes him from patriarchally hystericised forms of maternal
oppression (Lucía) to the mother (Pepa) whose nervous breakdown

signifies rupture from victimising constructions of subjectivity. If, in some ways, Carlos seems soft, co-operative, domesticated, that is because the film considers the days of macho masculinity to be numbered. He is indeed, as Lucía remarks towards the end of the film, guilty of treachery, but not really to her so much as to an ideology underlying the family structure that has led to his own and his natural mother's unhappiness.

Ultimately, while the film recognises that masculinity is in crisis, it never doubts the responsibility not just of Iván but of the patriarchal order as a whole for leading women to the brink of mental collapse. The crisis of masculinity spreads beyond Iván to the anonymous young man weeping on the balcony, Iván's subdued son Carlos, and the campy cabbie. But all of these characters are portrayed ambivalently: the tearful young man on the balcony enigmatically provides silent testimony to some deep-rooted melancholy; the Mambo taxi-driver, although in some ways an unthreatening alternative to the conventional male, providing a comic, cartoon-like focus for questioning the straighter norms of masculinity, is presented as a mass of hysterical consumerist pleasures and insecurities; Carlos, outwardly soft and sensitive, is nevertheless someone in whose stutter may be detected the signs of psychological imbalance; minor male characters like the police officers, often treated unceremoniously in other films by Almodóvar, comply with traditionally comic, even Pythonesque, standards of folly identified with bombastic or incompetent figures of authority. Through all of these characters masculinity is comically represented as also on the verge if not of nervous breakdown then at least of structural fatigue, exposed as a construction formed by decades of a macho culture which affects and constrains the lives of men as well as of women.

The film is not entirely devoid of moments that either gently ridicule or problematise women's subjectivity and desires. From the clownish cold-cream masks – reminiscent of Melanie Griffith's at one point in Jonathan Demme's *Something Wild* (1986) – on the faces of the women at the chemist where Pepa buys the sleeping pills, to the shrill voice – irreverently echoed by the soundtrack's borrowed Rimsky-Korsakov strains from 'Sheherezade' – of Cristina (Loles León), the telephone operator at the dubbing studio, to Ana's exploitation of her boyfriend, as she awaits an opportune moment to abandon him, to the silliness of the Shiite-terrorised Candela, or the authoritarian tendencies of Marisa and Paulina, the madness of Lucía, and the assertiveness of Pepa, the film gently suggests that men like Iván might well prefer to be on the run.

In some ways these are predominantly comic variants of a treatment of femininity given more problematic form in films such as *Tie Me Up, Tie Me Down*, *Matador* and *Kika*, where women are bound and gagged (*Tie Me Up, Tie Me Down*), demonised (*Matador*), or raped (*Kika*). At one level, and from some male perspectives, the female characters in *Women on the Verge* form a composite image of threatening otherness from whom there appears to be no escape. Even on TV, an Orwellian Big Sister or Big Mama is in a presiding role, displacing the patriarchal rule of Big Brother. (In a revealingly autobiographical sequence this role is played by Almodóvar's real mother, Francisca Caballero, a woman well past middle age, who is in part used to satirise the cult of the glamorous female.) These details reflect Iván's ambivalence towards femininity and motherhood – which simultaneously symbolise the origin of life, the object of desire as well as of separation anxiety, of dread as well as of envy, the guarantor of the male's narcissistic project to seek confirmation of self-sufficiency, potency and superiority as well as a threat to this project.

This ambivalence is also found in Almodóvar's meditations on what he considers to be women's greater capacity for tears:

I believe women cry better than men. That's why it's *Women on the Verge of a Nervous Breakdown* and not *Men on the Verge of a Nervous Breakdown*. ... I'm not going to deny that we boys suffer,

**and that loneliness affects us as much as a feminist, but who wants
to make a film these days about that? Not me, for sure. Girls, they're
the ones who know how to behave when they're abandoned by their
boyfriends. They are strangers to discretion, to a sense of the
ridiculous, to that horrible thing that used to be known as 'amour
propre'.**

(Villaverde, 1988)

These are the remarks of a man who knows his Sirk, himself no
apologist for repression and a director committed to the fullest
expression of feeling. Nevertheless, even though the causes of
unhappiness indisputably lie in *Women on the Verge* with the insensitive
male, these are not simply counteracted by finding inspiration in
female suffering.

If Iván has played a key role in destroying Lucía's inner
composure, her father's influence over her life sums up the film's
anxieties about the failure of conformist parents to provide a suitable
environment for the development of their child's self-sufficiency.
We suspect that Lucía, like many of Spain's Franco or post-Franco
children – to borrow Marsha Kinder's phrase (1983) – is, through the
failure of parenting, already prepared for lunacy well before she meets
Iván, even though medical diagnosis and certification of her condition
occur only after their romantic attachment. Victoria Secunda's remarks
on what she calls the 'Doting Father' help clarify the spell under which
women like Lucía are often condemned to lead their lives. The Doting
Father makes it almost impossible for a daughter to become self-
controlled and motivated in maturity, since she mistrusts her own
judgment and constantly seeks the approval either of her real father or
father-substitutes when making important decisions. This blurring of the
boundaries between parent and offspring reflects as much the latter's
dependence as the failure of the former's autonomy. The result is:

**Such fathers can become Bad Daddies in either of two ways: by
infantilising their daughters, beguiling them into lifelong**

dependency; or by objectifying them, flattering their daughters into giving them a material kind of love.

(Secunda,1993: 106)

Both tendencies of the Doting Father are discernible in attitudes expressed towards his daughter by Lucía's father. The subtleties of full psychoanalytic enquiry are avoided in the film, but Almodóvar gives the audience a glimpse of the power and dependence structures beyond the façade of conventional sweetness and favour surrounding their relationship.

Played by Julieta Serrano, an actress on whose controlled, acerbic persona Almodóvar relies elsewhere (in *Pepi, Luci, Bom, Dark Habits, Matador, Tie Me Up, Tie Me Down*), Lucía first appears in the film positioned in the frame against a background *mise en scène* that includes displays of dead butterflies. She is – like the Victoria Abril part in *Tie Me Up, Tie Me Down* – a collector's item boxed in the stifling atmosphere of conventional family life. Her 60s look of short skirts, pastel shades, kohled and droopy eyes, pale lips and back-combed hairstyles further signifying her retardment; she has become an object of display for a man who in his treatment of his daughter betrays the instincts more of a lepidoptorist than of a father. Where many contemporary Hollywood romantic comedies – such as *Peggy Sue Got Married* (Francis Ford Coppola, 1986) – use the 60s as a way of romanticising the past, contrasting present malaise with past vitality, a Spanish film can only realistically think of the same decade as a time of either mindless frivolity (as exemplified in the type of films made by Ozores and Lazaga) or, more sinisterly, of Franquist authoritarianism. This double-edged treatment of 60s attitudes and styles even extends both to the way in which Ana, the biker's sexy, taciturn dolly-bird, recalls in looks the leather-clad Marianne Faithful of *Girl on a Motorcycle* (Jack Cardiff, 1968) and to the symbolism of Iván's choice of Stockholm as a destination for his assignation with Paulina. In 60s Spain, Sweden was shorthand for sex, the cradle of liberated blondes and inspiration for the fantasies of Franco-repressed males whose cravings were given lurid form in the seemingly endless stream of comedies directed by Lazaga or Ozores (as well as, for example, Manuel Summers). The decade perfectly reflects the regime's double standards: while official ideology portrayed the country as a bastion of traditional morality – in sharp contrast to the looser attitudes of other European, and particularly Nordic, countries – men like Iván felt under no obligation to modify their treatment of women accordingly. From one point of view, the relationship between Iván and Lucía – especially in its contempt for the legitimating processes of marriage – acknowledges a characteristic refusal by ordinary men and women to be regimented into social conformism. From another, it draws attention to the ease with which women like Lucía – not trained for independence – often became, in their search for exclusive self-definition and fulfilment through men and an ideology of romantic love, victimised not just by the counterfeit ardour of shallow suitors but also by the ideological processes that nourished them.

Lucía's 60s clothes, hairstyles and cosmetics satisfy Almodóvar's taste for kitsch, while simultaneously offering him an opportunity for a figurative representation of ideological retardment. Significantly, though, while her mother would prefer Lucía to cast off these mementoes of a probably best-forgotten decade in the recent history of Spain, to move forward and out of the fixations of the past, her father encourages and indulges that retardment:

Father: This way I have the impression that time hasn't passed.
Mother: Well, I'm afraid to have to tell you that it has passed.
Father: Don't be a pain Carmen. Let her wear what she wants to.
Mother: That's right. Spoil her. So that she won't ever be cured.
Lucía: Do you like the way I look?
Father: You look great.
Lucía: How well you lie, Papa. That's why I love you.

More oppressed by the Franquist past, the mother urges her daughter to move with the times; more privileged by that past, the father nostalgically indulges his daughter's time-warped fantasies. Caught between the two of them, the daughter, in a flash of self-knowledge, knows she has been victimised by the deceptions of patriarchal culture, and that she has no alternative other than to continue to live as a psychological cripple, trapped by the self-mutilating fantasies spawned by her father's approbation.

The daughter here, to use psychoanalytic terms (Dio Bleichmar, 1995), is defined by the way in which her body serves as a screen on to which to project the coveted provocative sexuality. The female child – and in a sense Lucía is still a child – has learnt to see herself, her body, as a site for the look of the adult male (who in the first place is her father), a look that is sexually determined, and one that succeeds in

Marisa (Rossy de Palma), Almodóvar's postmodernist prima donna

internalising the girl/woman's sense of her body's projected sexuality, *agent provocateur* of male desire. Oedipalised to the point of dependence, Lucía turns herself through dress and cosmetics into a spectacle, not just to satisfy her own bizarre needs but also, in common with many other women, for the gratification and pleasure of others, especially her father and his ideological heir, Iván. This father sees in his daughter perhaps not just an independent person in her own right but, additionally, his ideal of femininity and a surrogate for the wife who may no longer much resemble the woman he married. Significantly, some, or perhaps all, of Lucía's 60s clothes once belonged, as she herself confesses, to her mother.

The father/daughter relationship in *Women on the Verge* recalls Hollywood treatments of the same subject in comedies such as Minnelli's *Father of the Bride* (1950) and *Father's Little Dividend* (1951), their modern remakes, *Father of the Bride* (Charles Shyer, 1991) and *Father of the Bride 2* (Charles Shyer, 1995), and Howard Hawks' *Monkey Business* (1952). In all of these films the special relationship between father and daughter extends beyond a father's natural love for his offspring to the point where his own youth and ideals are caught up in his desire to prevent her from reaching maturity and the pursuit of independence. Lucía's father's approval of her 60s-fixated look is the equivalent of George's disapproval of his daughter's wedding plans in the *Father of the Bride* films, or the Cary Grant character's courtship of the youthful Marilyn Monroe character and estrangement from his wife (Ginger Rogers) in *Monkey Business.*

Like Pepa, though, but in much more wayward and disturbed forms, Lucía attempts to abandon passivity for activity. Having finally discovered the truth about his relationship with Pepa, whom he has abandoned for Paulina, Lucía heads for the airport, determined to kill Iván. Predictably, Almodóvar follows Lucía's tormented quest for her old lover through a mixture of farce and melodrama. The incongruity of her dark intentions and unlikely means of transport – riding pillion on a hijacked motorcycle – is matched by scenes at the airport itself where as she mounts the escalator the camera is placed in such a way as to make only her head visible, as if severed from the rest of her body. This comic-horror shot of Lucía's mutilation unfolds against a background of musical effects recalling in their screechy sounds the violin-dominated score for the shower scene in Hitchcock's *Psycho*. But while *Psycho* concentrates on the effects of a son disturbed by his mother's possessiveness, the stress in *Women on the Verge* lies on the daughter/mother's dementia, reflecting in close-up another of Hitchcock's themes, that of the castrating mother driven towards madness (as in *Strangers on a Train*) or domestic tyranny (as in *Notorious*, 1946) by the social and psychological effects of a patriarchal culture. Having failed at the airport to shoot dead her former lover, Lucía the daughter cries out that she wishes to be taken to her home, the 'López Ibor' clinic, a remark of obviously intentional ambiguity. The plea to officials swarming all around her at the airport expresses Lucía's desire to be literally returned to the 'hospital' – an establishment that exists even today in Madrid – and also hints at a possible identification between the clinic and her family home, a suggestion that draws a meaningful parallel between both places. The point about this deliberate pairing is that Juan José López Ibor, the founder of the clinic, was a psychiatrist – never, in any case, a sympathetic figure in Almodóvar's films, as may be judged for instance by the antics of the female Argentinian psychiatrist in *Labyrinth of Passions* – of what might be called the Vatican school of psychiatry. A member of Opus Dei, a highly influential conservative religious order that enjoyed much power under Franco, López Ibor could be said in those days to have practised a strictly reactionary form of psychiatry.

Lucía, then, like many women of her generation, is trapped inside a patriarchal labyrinth, her inner life enclosed within layers of neatly fitting family and institutional structures. The family here, unlike its Utopian representation in pro-establishment sub-Capraesque 60s films like *La gran familia / The Great Family* (Fernando Palacios, 1962), *La familia y uno más / The Family Plus One* (Fernando Palacios, 1965) and

La familia bien, gracias / The Family's Fine, Thanks (Pedro Masó, 1979),
is dysfunctional, a site of alienation and manipulation, where Lucía's
mind and body have been set at odds with each other, reflecting, in
Foucault's terms (1991), the negative effects of the power structures by
which she is trapped. Significantly, on the other hand, Pepa, the woman
who finally succeeds in taking control of her own destiny, never
mentions her parents, or her family background. Not pressurised by
her parents, she can lead a more independent, neurosis-free life that
provides a stark contrast to Lucía's, whose father's masterly voice lives
on to a certain extent in Iván. The film is full of nice ironies: Pepa, freer
than Lucía, will be able eventually to liberate herself from the mesmeric
power of Iván's voice heard on the answerphone; Lucía, older and less
liberated than Pepa, also hears Iván's voice in recordings, through his
role as dubbing actor, but since she has become so institutionalised
by the legacy of *Franquismo*, something given literal form through her
certified insanity, she remains trapped by the tyrannies of the past.

The seductive, bewitching voice of her former lover provoking
her into drastic, demented action is also a voice shaped by her father
and by López Ibor, figures of authority whose rhetoric is as equivocal
as the lines spoken by the returning hero played by Sterling Hayden
in *Johnny Guitar*. The point is made through the lyrics of two boleros
that open and close the film, proving once again that Almodóvar's
work is characterised almost as much by its music as by, say, its
comic–melodramatic camp sensibility, or by its dependence on Carmen
Maura, Victoria Abril or Antonio Banderas. Different traditions of music
are raided to consolidate the emotional intensity of sexual relationships.
The Law of Desire, and its narrative of a young man's (Antonio
Banderas) obsessive and eventually fatal love for another man (Eusebio
Poncela) for example, would simply not be the same film without the
plangent lyrics and melody of one of the Panchos' most famous boleros,
'Lo dudo' ('I wonder'). Almodóvar defines the bolero as 'the most
perfect, most direct way of expressing what I want to say' (1991: 145).
In other films the music of 'zarzuelas' (Spanish operetta), 'tonadillas'

and other types of popular song adds an essential dimension of lyricism or drama to the narrative.

Women on the Verge often feels like a musical, invoking not only *Funny Face* but also the full range and varied traditions of the genre both in Hollywood and in Spain, using known melodies or original sounds to vary perspective, to emphasise, reformulate or violate formal or thematic patterns. Among the film's most striking examples of musical counterpoint are the introductory and concluding songs. The first, 'Soy infeliz' ('I'm unhappy'), sung by Lola Beltrán (music by Ventura Romero), immediately sets the film's tone of resignation through its sceptical treatment of love and the futility of attempts to revive the flames of extinct desire, perfectly summarising the narrative ahead:

Soy infeliz	**I'm unhappy**
porque sé que no me quieres,	**Because I know you don't love me.**
¿para qué más insistir?	**Why go on?**
Vive feliz mi bien.	**Be happy my love**
Si el amor que tu me diste	**because I'll always feel**
para siempre he de sentir.	**the love you gave me.**

Its mood of melancholy resignation is reprised, more cynically, in the concluding bolero, 'Teatro' ('Theatre'), sung by La Lupe in a forceful and resonant Eartha Kitt-like voice:

Igual que en un escenario	**As in a play,**
finges tu dolor barato.	**you fake your cheap pain.**
Tu drama no es necesario.	**Your drama is unnecessary.**
Yo conozco este teatro.	**I know it's only theatre.**

In its stress on the theatricality of subjectivity the song offers a memorable example of the tradition of the bolero as a genre eliding sweet harmonies and bitter lyrics. Masculinity here – as exemplified by Iván – has presented itself as finally no more than a seductive spectacle, a theatre of broken dreams and desires, a confection of images projected for the purpose of exploitation rather than as a celebration of redemption through love. The film explores the extent to which appearance substitutes for or colonises subjectivity, making relations between the sexes seem like nothing more than the shadow-play of imagery:

Teatro, lo tuyo es puro teatro,	**Theatre, that's all you are,**
falsedad bien empleada,	**well-played falsehood,**
estudiado simulacro.	**studied pretence.**
Fue tu mejor actuación	**Your best role was**
destrozar mi corazón.	**to destroy my heart,**
Y hoy que me lloras de veras	**and now that you're really crying**
recuerdo tu simulacro.	**I recall your pretence.**

The dementia of women caused by male theatricality is given its most tragic representation in Lucía, and its most comic variant in the casting of María Barranco as Candela, the unwitting Shiite terrorist's moll. Since her earliest part in an Almodóvar film (*What Have I Done to Deserve This?*) María Barranco has established herself as a leading comic actress in the Spanish cinema, her slightly gawky appearance, Andalusian accent and air of distraction making her highly suited to the role of Candela in *Women on the Verge*. Here all of these farcical qualities are stressed even further. Whereas Lucía's age and status as a woman of leisure are given as major reasons for her condition as a potential victim, it is Candela's Andalusian origins which mark the spot of her vulnerability. In Spain, Andalusian women are recognised as being among the most traditional. The reasons lie perhaps largely in the historically rural character of the region, a still under-industrialised part of the country where the impact of Moorish culture has faded least (Sánchez Ochoa et al., 1992). Candela represents comically the Andalusian woman's firmer embrace of domesticity. Even Candela's career as an actress identifies her early on through the contraceptive advertisement as more defined by marriage and the home than by career and independence. Clothes, jewellery and cosmetics immediately establish Candela's vulnerability: her blue-and-white striped, tight-fitting mini-skirt, knee-length white stockings, together with her boyishly cropped hair, seem more like the matchday strip used by a lanky defender playing for Barranco's real-life hometown football club, Malaga F.C., than the garb of a sophisticated cosmopolitan. Yet this apparent flirtation with transsexualism has more of the air of youthful innocence than of sexual dissidence, a suspicion further stressed by those characteristic coffeepot earrings, emphasising, as they swing about her face in the film's early scenes, her agitated state of mind. Like the pseudo-football strip, the earrings are signs of childishness (no expensive conventional Tiffany's jewellery here), and, given Almodóvar's known

Funny Face (Stanley Donen, 1957), and fashion-magazine aesthetics

taste for Doris Day films, emblems too of Pop Art's celebration of the consumerist ethos, or perhaps even more significantly, of the traditional Andalusian woman's identification with domesticity, private spaces and cookery.

Even so, Candela's character is complex, and to some extent her appearances in early scenes are an ironic projection of the colonisation of the female mind and body by the *mise en scène* of the house. Good clean living, family unity and the idealisation of romance, so characteristic of 50s style (Horn, 1993: 46), are wittily recalled here. Candela, whom we never see cooking or sewing in the stereotypically Andalousian way, has after all left home, become a model and actress, and has taken a lover – all actions she can tell Pepa about but which she would never have confessed to her parents. But the childish, unprotected aura of the provincial girl vulnerable to the dangers of the metropolis remains, even though she begins to relax and fall under the spell of the more resourceful Pepa in the all-female flat. Her clothes – exterior signs of her cultural and social positioning – change, an adolescent style yielding to the more mature look of long black skirt that registers, in addition, her mourning for an innocence lost to the Shiite terrorist lover. Significantly too, the black skirt belongs to Pepa: through this detail Almodóvar reinforces the mutual fate of two victims of terrorism, while simultaneously drawing attention to the way in which Candela finally acquires some of Pepa's strength.

Almodóvar's verbal wit is often at its sharpest in Candela's casual remarks: 'Men take advantage of me. Look how I've been treated by the Arab world.' Like Buñuel – in, for instance, *That Obscure Object of Desire* (1977) – he treats terrorists ambivalently: on the positive side, they are part of the text's subversion of established order; on the negative side, they make no distinctions between deserving and undeserving targets. Almodóvar's style here is camp: an inferior, humorous form of discourse includes commentary on a key political issue, where a low-order item (betrayal in love) is set against a higher one (worldwide terrorism), in a style very similar to Woody Allen's

(Babington and Evans, 1989: 156). The difference is that the joke is told here not by a practised joke-teller, but by an ingenue, her remark acquiring camp rather than straightforwardly comic significance in delivery.

The brilliant treatment of both Candela and Lucía, the former terrorised by political the latter by psychological demons, emphasises the extent to which Almodóvar has striven to create a coherent and versatile ensemble of minor characters, none of whom is restricted to mere arbitrariness. This was the film in which Almodóvar moved from gratuitousness towards coherence in patterns involving minor as well as major characters. And while the concierge, Candela and the other women contribute towards creating a complex image of the varied but related social constructions of female subjectivity, so the minor male characters – Carlos, the Mambo taxi-driver and the others – all offer different perspectives on the crisis of post-Franco forms of masculinity. In *Women on the Verge* men and women are in conflict, ignorant of each other, mutually hostile and sometimes even murderous. But the two groups are nevertheless interdependent, locked into the same needs and destinies.

The flat is a fantasy space for renewal and transformation

4 Carmen Maura

Johnny: They should have lived happily ever after.
Vienna: They didn't. They broke up. He couldn't see himself tied
down to a home.
Johnny Guitar (Nicholas Ray, 1954)

Explaining the original idea behind *Women on the Verge*, Almodóvar has
remarked: 'I thought of giving myself an overdose of Carmen Maura, to
make a film only with her in it and to see how far we could go' (Strauss,
1995: 91). Although the plan came to nothing there is a sense in which
Women on the Verge nevertheless remains mainly hers. As a result, she
has been predominantly identified with this film, to the extent that the
British release of the video of *¡Ay Carmela!* (Carlos Saura, 1990) has a
reference on its cover to Carmen Maura as the star of *Women on the
Verge*. While *Women on the Verge* is full of marvels, everything is
overshadowed by the electrifying presence of Carmen Maura. Very
different from her successors as the Almodóvar leading lady – the elfin
Victoria Abril (*Tie Me Up, Tie Me Down, High Heels, Kika*) and the
haggard Marisa Paredes (*High Heels, The Flower of My Secret*) – Carmen
Maura remains the quintessentially Almodovarian 'comedienne': comic,
tragic, warm, spirited, resilient and flawed, a hybrid heroine forever
poised between comedy and melodrama.

Making her first appearance as a 'chica Almodóvar' in *Pepi, Luci,
Bom*, she went on to star in five more films, *Women on the Verge* proving
to be her last, after a bitter row with Almodóvar (since patched up)
during the Oscars ceremony when it was nominated for best foreign film.
Even critics not especially sympathetic either to Almodóvar's comedy
of excess, or his comic book characterisations, have had to acknowledge
the dynamic contribution to *Women on the Verge* of Carmen Maura,
whose Pepa rescues the representation of women from the Richard
Avedon two-dimensionality of *Funny Face* (Stanley Donen, 1957) so
strikingly invoked at the beginning of the film (O'Toole, 1988: 271).

Surprisingly, Maura has only painful memories even of the filming, well before the public disagreement in Hollywood, and of discovering for the first time that she was no longer in harmony with the man who had catapulted her to stardom: 'For me it was a very sad, anxious time. I had never had such a bad time before' (Ponga, 1993: 99).

Carmen Maura's career could be aptly summarised by her early TV appearance as Melibea, a part described by Salvador de Madariaga in a voice-over commentary for the programme as the representation not of corrupted innocence but of female self-discovery. A key character in Fernando de Rojas' *La Celestina* (1499), one of the great literary texts of the Spanish Golden Age, Melibea is a portrait of a woman challenging stereotypical categorisation based on ideals of courtly perfection or devillish wantonness.[16] The part is an apt fictional parallel for an actress

often cast in roles dramatising women's attempts to struggle free of the legacy of *Franquismo*, embracing the new opportunities offered under democracy (as in, for instance, *Cómo ser infeliz y disfrutarlo / How to Be*

Pepa recalls *Johnny Guitar*'s Vienna (Joan Crawford)

Unhappy and Enjoy It (Enrique Urbizu, 1993)). Even though in her playing of Melibea – the daughter defying conventional and parental authority – Maura's persona is to some extent subordinate to contemporary standards of fashion, her forcefulness remains largely uncompromised. As a 60s Melibea she submits to the processes of ritualised feminisation, her eyebrows plucked almost without trace, her pallor and demureness more symptomatic of the decade's Botticelli-induced norms of femininity than perhaps of her own tastes or tendencies. Described by Nigel Floyd, as an 'earthy beauty' bringing 'flesh and blood reality to her roles' (1991), she has indeed, since her fledgling TV and film roles, become identified, as she herself recognises, with *'papeles de mujer fuerte y de armas tomar'* (that is, strong women roles) often earning comparisons with Anna Magnani, Jeanne Moreau and Hanna Schygulla, all of whom were at their best playing characters under pressure, reflecting the experience of women leading adverse, recognisable lives.

These qualities have been stressed by Almodóvar himself in remarks about Maura's performance in *The Law of Desire*. In *Patty Diphusa and Other Texts* which includes a short story about an outrageous porn star, Almodóvar discusses ambiguities of gender, something most convincingly represented, he feels, in the characterisation of Scarlett O'Hara. In the course of this discussion he makes a direct reference to Maura's performance in *The Law of Desire*:

Beyond the Circus-like joke about transvestism, Carmen's mimicry is extraordinary. Maura shows she is in possession of such a variety of registers that she turns her work into a true festival. This woman grows in front of the camera ... amusing, pathetic, muscular, ambiguous, paranoid. Tina Quintero, thanks to Carmen Maura, is my most complete portrayal of a woman to date
(Almodóvar, 1991: 101–2).

In *Women on the Verge,* however, the initial comparison made in the film

via Pepa's dubbing of Vienna in *Johnny Guitar* is between Carmen
Maura and Joan Crawford, both playing women jilted by their lovers.
As Terenci Moix's grandmother accurately puts it in *El peso de la paja /
Weighing the Straw* – his brilliant film-laden autobiography about a
childhood in and around Barcelona in the 40s and 50s – Joan Crawford
was the actress in a suit, often cast in roles compelling her to choose
between career and romance (1990: 306). *Mildred Pierce* (Michael
Curtiz, 1945), *Daisy Kenyon* (Otto Preminger, 1947), *Queen Bee* (Ranald
MacDougall, 1955), *The Best of Everything* (Jean Negulesco, 1959) and
Johnny Guitar, for instance, all show her moving between the private and
the public, taking men on, not as performer or love-interest, but as
professional competitor or partner, in the traditionally male preserves of
business, enterprise or, in the case of *Johnny Guitar*, of Western saloon

Johnny Guitar

management. The comparison with Crawford is instructive. Although Almodóvar says he adored Ava Gardner (who is honoured both directly and indirectly in *Matador*) and claims he would have loved above all to have worked with Bette Davis or Katharine Hepburn, *Women on the Verge* celebrates Crawford, largely perhaps because of her initially surprising resemblance to Carmen Maura.

The allusion works in a number of ways. Although Crawford has a steelier edge – something borne out, of course, by the documented revelations in her daughter's biography, *Momie Dearest*, concerning her obsessive relationship with her adopted children – the star meanings of both actresses seem remarkably complementary, especially vis-à-vis female subjectivity and the relations between the sexes. The major difference, of course, is that Crawford's struggles took place against a background of conservative attitudes towards gender and sexuality, while Maura has done her best work in the far freer climate of a country exorcising the inhibitions and repressions of its recent past. Yet, despite the constraints of the largely conformist decades in which she was a star, like many of her contemporaries, Crawford was often larger or more radical than the films in which she appeared, a point whose general significance is emphasised in much recent theorising of female stars, in recognition not only of the stresses and strains of classical Hollywood films but also of the implications, above all for female spectatorship, of identification between restrictedly dissident females and largely conformist texts.

Since Richard Dyer brought attention to the relations between star, film, industry and the social definitions of subjectivity, star study has progressed towards analysis of mechanisms related to identification, pleasure and desire. Here too, as Christine Gledhill (1991) and others have argued, there has been a gradual shift from theories closely modelled on Lacanian psychoanalysis, where the construction of the ideal spectator reproduces patterns related to the construction of the gendered subject in language, towards discussion of the tensions between the processes of audience identification and the ideological positioning or 'interpellation' (Althusser, 1977) of the spectator. In touching on such matters, especially in considerations of the female star as fetish, it is salutary to remember Jacky Stacy's references to sources of inspiration enjoyed by women spectators through identification with strong actresses of the 30s, 40s and 50s, as well as to her suspicion of any single-positioning theory of spectatorship which collapses differences of sex, class, ethnicity, or sexual orientation, and in which female spectators are only able to derive pleasure from a film either through masculinisation (Mulvey, 1975) or marginalisation (Doane, 1988). As Gledhill also argues, stars mediate rather than reflect meanings or ideals of subjectivity.

Despite the constraints of the day, Joan Crawford offered women spectators, through her forceful presence, an outlet for their own

The women's man-free flat in *How to Marry a Millionaire* (Jean Negulesco, 1953)

frustrations and desires. In a different country and culture, in a transitional period moving from dictatorship to democracy, Maura parallels Crawford in giving Spanish women an equally potent source of vicarious fulfilment. Paul Julian Smith has already drawn attention to the way in which, above all in *Women on the Verge,* Almodóvar created women characters liberated from the role models available in Franquist-inspired manuals on femininity extolling the virtues of good housekeeping, cookery, sewing, healthy exercise and domesticity (1994: 105). And although she is not the only actress in Spain in recent years to have embodied new ideals of womanhood, Carmen Maura personifies those ideals – whether in films by Almodóvar or by other directors – with drive and conviction. Yet the success of women stars like Carmen Maura, Charo López, Ana Belén, or Mercedes Sampietro, all of whom rose to prominence in more relaxed political times, should not lessen the impact of an earlier generation of actresses who despite the often tawdry material of the films in which they appeared nevertheless managed to represent women in more than trivial ways. In the field of comedy, Concha Velasco and Gracita Morales, for instance, often managed to rise above the mediocrity of their scripts, the former a sort of sexually liberated Doris Day, the latter a squeaky-voiced soubrette, each in her own way affronting stereotype, forcing her individuality through layers of banality.

Concha Velasco and Gracita Morales reached their peak largely before the end of dictatorship (Velasco is still very popular, currently featuring in a TV series, *Yo una mujer / I, a Woman,* about a traditional middle-class mother and wife who undergoes a mid-life crisis, taking control of her life, abandoning family, children and home). Carmen Maura, who to some extent inherits their legacy as forceful comediennes, had the good fortune to reach her peak in democracy. After her initial faltering steps in TV and cabaret (as early as 1969), she made her first real impression, precisely at the moment when the *ancien régime* was on the point of collapse, as a *'progre'* (progressive) actress in *comedias madrileñas* (Madrid comedies) made by Fernando Colomo and

Félix Rotaeta. Despite her denials of any offscreen involvement with
'progres' – 'I was never very *progre* . . . I felt out of place' (Ponga, 1993:
61) – the effect of her association with these directors, especially
Colomo, as well as her much publicised divorce (involving the loss of
custody of her two children) and her self-confessed transformation from
well-to-do Sloane Ranger equivalent, running an art gallery in Madrid,
to more relaxed, self-assured metropolitan, led to an inevitable
identification with so-called progressive groups and unorthodox
lifestyles. Separation from her children and husband, after five years of
marriage, seemed inevitable for a woman so strongly drawn to acting:

**[W]hen the moment comes to say goodbye, to take all your things
away, it's very hard, and more so if you have two children. But after
five minutes into my performance at the theatre, I'd already calmed
down. When I had to recall everything for the legal processes of
separation, my friend Teresa Pellicer had to help me because I no
longer remembered anything about my marriage. It had vanished
from my mind.**

    (Ponga, 1993: 49)

Her comic and melodramatic work in the *comedias madrileñas*, as
well as her association with political radicals, paved the way for her
development as the actress who in Almodóvar's films truly came to
represent for women a decisive break with the past.

    In *¿Qué hace una chica como tú en un sitio como éste? / What's a
Girl like You Doing in a Place like This?* (Fernando Colomo, 1978),
fact and fiction converge. In 1975 Carmen Maura had been raped
by a career soldier. Her way of dealing with this trauma was through
pardoning the rapist and refusing to take advantage of a legal system
that had only recently been sentencing political activists to death, while
exorcising the incident itself through an invitation to a friend to '*echar
un polvo*' (screw) in the same bed where the outrage had taken place
(Ponga, 1993: 56). In *What's a Girl like You Doing in a Place like This?*,

the Maura character is raped, by her own husband, and, as in life, seeks
the event's obliteration from memory through the seduction, in her own
flat, of an admirer. Scenes like this quickly identified Maura as an
independent woman, taking control of her own body and sexuality.
Maura's identification with sexual initiative and assertiveness became
even more pronounced in her work with Almodóvar.

**Colomo's *progre* world was like a convent school compared with
Almodóvar and his friends. I was guilt personified and Pedro helped
me a great deal in freeing me from my guilt complexes and other
even sillier complexes like worrying about my belly or big breasts**
(Ponga, 1993: 64).

Her persona in the Almodóvar films reflects through the generic drives
of both comedy and melodrama the liberation as well as the continued
repression of women in democracy. Maura's expression is a blend of
affirmation and bitterness. If the typical 60s heroine struggles against
Franquist tracts on femininity, the post-60s heroine exemplified by
Maura seeks definition through the political agenda of the women's
movement, the Instituto de la Mujer (Women's Institute) and the kind
of writing on sex and gender represented, for instance, by Lidia Falcón,
one of Spain's leading feminist theorists, in books like *Mujer y poder
político / Women and Political Power* (1992). No direct relationship is
implied here; nor is there a suggestion that the films in any way
consciously seek to rehearse the polemics of post-dictatorship sexual
politics. Indeed, Maura herself refers to an episode of her extremely
popular TV show, *Esta Noche* (Tonight) in which she was rebuked by
Lidia Falcón for appearing to criticise feminists for not having a sense
of humour (Ponga, 1993: 73). Lidia Falcón's cool reception of Maura's
remarks points to an important undercurrent running through the
Maura persona. Her New Woman character, especially in the Almodóvar
films, remains ultimately approachable: for all their power and energy,
for all their iconoclasm and wildness, her Tinas and Pepas are either too

compromised by their heritage or too seduced by the lure of the mainstream to seek radical marginalisation. Like the TV presenter in *Esta Noche*, they are too socialised for alienation:

I tried not to make that girl aggressive, getting her to talk in a relaxed way with the audience, as if she were addressing a single spectator, someone with whom the audience could identify themselves, whom they would like

(Ponga, 1993: 73).

In the cluster of films she made between *Pepi, Luci, Bom* and *Women on the Verge,* the 'chica Almodóvar', for all her defiance, remains constrained by generic convention, her comic or melodramatic or

The oneiric landscape of Pepa's flat

comic–melodramatic roles creating a set of expectations in the audience
that rule out uncompromising refusal or marginalisation. The use of
her maternal maiden name (in Spain married women retain their family
names, both the paternal and the maternal) perfectly mirrors this
indecisiveness over conformism or transgression. In rejecting her
paternal maiden name she identifies herself with a matrilineal heritage;
but as the surname was that of her maternal grandfather, a famous
general, the patriarchal aura survives. This pattern of assertiveness
suborned by complaisance even marks her physical appearance.

The Maura look in these films – and even more recently in *Pareja
de tres / Three's a Couple* (1995) or *El palomo cojo / The Crippled Pigeon*
(Armiñán, 1995), and *Hay amores que matan / There Are Deadly Affairs*
(1996) – mixes pathos with comedy. The ever-present fringe (without
which she confesses she would never risk being seen in public) suggests
not only a cosmetic strategy for camouflaging an over-expansive
forehead, but also vulnerability, a defensive gesture made in readiness
for life's surprises. Even the slightly crooked teeth and heavy chin
express more than unfeminine aggression. Where necessary, they
function ambivalently either to project the pathos of victimisation
(especially in *What Have I Done to Deserve This?*) or else, comically, to
offset the more regular features reflecting norms of feminine beauty
demanded by contemporary fashions. Her beauty now, though, is
painted not with fine but thick brushstrokes. Vanished are the delicate
lines of a Renaissance profile, replaced by a look at once more natural
and less deferential. So in the Almodóvar films, and ever since, one is
struck not only by an almost Kleinian, monstrously feminine mouth, but
also by eyes as enormous as a cyclops', their mascared lashes, severely
pencilled lids and dark, unplucked Crawfordesque brows vividly
seeming to proclaim woman's appropriation of the gaze, constructing a
look made all the more dramatic through the effect of her invariable
choices of red for her costumes. Recent films like *Baton rouge* (Rafael
Moleón, 1988), *Chatarra / Scrap* (Felix Rotaeta, 1991), *La reina anónima /
The Anonymous Queen* (Gonzalo Suárez, 1992), *El palomo cojo* and

Pareja de tres, all at some moment reveal her as a Lady in Red – a colour, as Almodóvar himself remarks, of passion and vitality, and additionally intended in *Women on the Verge* to invoke the meanings of the *femme fatale* (Strauss, 1995: 100).

For, in some ways, of course, *Women on the Verge*'s Pepa is a comic variant of the tragic, flaming man-killer (Kael, 1988: 97), albeit in designer Juan Gatti's camp mode inspired by Richard Avedon styles. The opening credits, so reminiscent of *Funny Face,* highlight in their fetishistic mutilations of the female body the superficialities of femininity, prioritising cosmetics and fashion at the expense of more durable realities. This collage of striking images defines women above all through narcissistic self-preoccupation.

But as the visual rhetoric surrounding Carmen Maura in *Women*

on the Verge heavily relies on the aesthetics of Pop, so Pepa is governed to a certain extent by a sensibility branded above all by pastiche, exaggeration and bathos, and an inflected persona perfectly exemplifying

Pepa makes friends with her lover's son Carlos; the telephone motif recalls Cocteau's *La Voix humaine* and Almodóvar's days at the Telephone Exchange

the film's awareness of the inauthentic surface-thin texture of the new
consumerist society's cosmeticised, glossy constructions of subjectivity.
The film again takes its cue here from *Funny Face*, a Cinderella narrative
where the Audrey Hepburn character is transformed from librarian
dowdiness into fashion-model glamour, and where Fred Astaire is
reminded by a colleague, 'You belong to the fashion world. Face it, we're
a cold lot – artificial and totally lacking in sentiment.' The ambivalent
ethos of 50s (and 60s) Pop is reproduced and refocused for late 80s
Spain, a country where hedonism and consumerism – sustained by
political scandal which finally led in 1996 to the collapse of Felipe
Gonzaléz' Socialist government after thirteen years in power – threaten
to colonise its soul. *Women on the Verge*'s Pop Art ambience recalls both
the blown-up comic style of artists like Roy Lichtenstein, caricaturing

Pepa pursues the elusive Iván

human emotions through huge close-ups of the human body, and the more directly satirical treatment of consumerism associated with the work of Andy Warhol. Characteristically, Almodóvar's approach in *Women on the Verge* is equivocal, now fascinated by glossy surfaces, now weary of their insubstantiality. Alternately warm and cool, he defines his own position like this:

The aggressiveness of my films perhaps derives from the fact that I'm neither tender nor lyrical. I feel little affection for my characters, for my world, or even for myself.
(Boyero, 1981: 43–5)

As in the pictures of Lichtenstein and Warhol, objects in *Women on the Verge* are magnified (for instance, Maura's shoes as she paces up and down waiting to hear from Iván, or Iván's mouth as he speaks into the microphone, or the telephone itself), garish colours made to clash (the interiors of Pepa's flat, the lawyer's office, or the dubbing studio), and fashions fetishised (above all, Lucía's wardrobe). Through these blow-ups, riotous colours and patterns, extreme aestheticisation, complementing the drives of comedy, he distances the viewer from the film, offsetting melodramatic emotional involvement. Just as the campy cabbie is annexed by Pop – his orange hair, mambo music, effeminate tone of voice and consumerist decadence an affront to realism – so too is Carmen Maura enveloped by a Pop Art masquerade of femininity. As Pauline Kael remarked, 'she doesn't make a move that isn't stylised' (1988: 124).

In 'Womanliness as Masquerade', Joan Riviere (1966) discusses how a woman patient governed by 'masculine' desires both concealed and fulfilled those desires through the assumption of a mask of femininity. The highly aestheticised Carmen Maura look in *Women on the Verge* leads here not, as in the case referred to by Riviere (and in Almodóvar's *Pepi, Luci, Bom*), to speculation about lesbian sexuality, but to interrogation of the fundamental components of the new, late 80s consumerist society in Spain. From one point of view, Carmen Maura's highly colourful visual appearance in *Women on the Verge* contributes to the film's overall use of colour to commemorate release from past austerities; from another, as in Warhol's over-cosmeticisation of Elizabeth Taylor and Marilyn Monroe, tube skirts, high heels and colour augment the ambience of mask and counterfeit perhaps even more strikingly projected through Julieta Serrano's Jackie Kennedy-as-Wicked-Witch-of-the-West-crossed-with-Norman-Bates'-Mother's look as Lucía. In the film's press book Carmen Maura comments on the tight skirts and high heels demanded of her part as Pepa:

Of course they'll be uncomfortable, but I'll never show it. For someone like Pepa, high heels are one of the best ways to handle her suffering. If Pepa didn't keep up her looks, her spirits would break down completely. The art of coquetry is a discipline in itself and represents her main strength. It means that her problems have not yet got the best of her.

(Almodóvar, 1988: 8)

Maura's psychological analysis of Pepa's taste for chic styles is sharp: Pepa's inner turmoil fails to undermine her self-control. The perfect order of the outer self registers the assertiveness and dynamism of a woman who will eventually triumph over present woes. But Pepa's cosmetics, hairstyle and costume, belonging to the film's larger patterns of design and colour, also draw attention beyond the complexities of psychology to the determinants governing the construction of subjectivity itself. Both Lucía and Pepa take part in a masquerade of femininity, thus creating an effect of coolness and detachment, enabling the viewer more easily to note the extent to which femininity is defined through artifice and imagery. Carmen Maura's look recalls Alex Katz's 1963 picture, 'The Red Smile', in its awareness that the measure of femininity, and not only by men like Iván, is often determined, even in a late 80s European democracy, by luxury-item metaphysics.

5 Closure

I am intrigued by the playfulness, and the insincerity, of men. I think often of the connection between 'play' and 'please'.
Douglas Sirk

Through its prioritisation of Pepa's story, the film sharpens its critique of the concept of romantic love. Because it treads a careful balance between melodrama and comedy it avoids the pattern, so dominant in unequivocal romantic comedies – Hollywood or Spanish, conventional or unconventional – where initial antagonism between the main characters eventually yields to reconciliation and union. Right from the start in *Women on the Verge* the special quality of the happy couple, any happy couple, is placed in question. Pepa and Iván, Lucía and Iván, Candela and the Shiite, even Ana and Ambite, and Carlos and Marisa, are all couples whose relationships are seen to be in various degrees of crisis. Whereas traditional romantic comedies (from *Pillow Talk* to *Todos los hombres sois iguales*) may often acknowledge the difficulties, aggression, or vicissitudes of all relationships, even those that afflict the romantic couple, they do so in ways that ultimately succumb to more powerful affirmative drives that give their closures, with varying degrees of emphasis, a Utopian significance. *Women on the Verge*, too tainted by melodrama, has no such faith in human relationships. Like the Woody Allen character in *Annie Hall* who knows his brother is crazy to think he is a chicken but complains they will miss his eggs once he is sectioned, Almodóvar's characters recognise the folly as well as the necessity of investing so heavily in love. But like the Allen character who needs the eggs, Almodóvar's characters rarely learn from their mistakes. Even here, amid the debris of a flat whose virtual destruction (with its torched bed, broken glass and so on) reflects the havoc caused by a failed love-affair, Pepa remarks as she picks her way through the litter of bodies still drugged by gazpacho that she fancies the telephone repair man, adding with an afterthought that she had better leave him for Marisa who will be in greater need of him once she wakes up to discover that Carlos has transferred his affections to Candela. And yet, since *Women on the Verge* is much more acutely conscious of the disappointments than of the fulfilments of desire, perhaps the real reason Pepa leaves him for Marisa is in order to spare herself the inevitability of yet more heartache through love. Even if, as a result, our cravings for a happy ending are frustrated, even if we are denied the opportunity for vindicating our own lives through those of our surrogates on the screen, we may at least find some consolation in confronting not only our frailties in the crazed behaviour of characters like Iván, but also our strengths through Pepa's exhilarating triumph over adversity and her refusal to be victimised. Once she announces '*estoy harta de ser buena* / I've had enough of being good' and drops the sedatives into the gazpacho, we share her

The hysterical Andalusian Candela prefers suicide to Shiite reprisal

conviction that there is a limit to decency when one has been betrayed in love.

In this, the film departs somewhat from the traditions of melodrama, where, as Kathleen Rowe points out (1995), despite the centrality of the female, the genre's focus, whether in its conservative or radical variants, usually insists on the woman's eventual capitulation to external forces. Of course, even in *Women on the Verge* the ending is far from conclusive. We suspect that eventually the cosy sisterly scene with Marisa will lose its fascination for Pepa. And won't Marisa resent Carlos' attentions to Candela? Will Pepa, as soon as Iván has been forgotten, not find herself ruled once again by the laws of desire? For all its tidy stillness, the film's closure is inexpressibly ambiguous: with so many problems remaining unresolved, we are encouraged to wonder on whether the lure of the perverse will not eventually draw these characters as powerfully to their continuing destinies as other less enslaving modes of fulfilment.

Notes

1 The budget figure was given by Agustín Almodóvar in a private interview; for box-office receipts, see Instituto de Cinematografía y Artes Audiovisuales (1995: 18).

2 On Spain's gradual transformation from rural backwater to modern urban-dominated leading European nation, see Daniel Villaverde (1988).

3 See, for instance, Claesson (1980), Alvarez (1977), Gual (1982) and the 'El Mundo de la Pareja' (World of the Couple) series, for example *Cómo hacer feliz a su pareja* (How to Make Your Partner Happy) (Madrid: Planeta, 1983) and *25 Maneras de hacer el amor* (25 Ways to Make Love) (Madrid: Planeta, 1983). See also Goñi (1980).

4 For further information on censorship during the Franco régime, see Román Gubern (1980).

5 Almodóvar (1991: 11) refers to Dorothy Parker, to Anita Loos' heroine Lorelei, to Divine, to *Breakfast at Tiffany's* Holly Golightly and Fran Lebowitz as

sources of inspiration for his character Patty Diphusa. These precursors, as well as the wider range of Hollywood and Spanish references to film comedy and melodrama, clearly also play into the characterisation of *Women on the Verge*.

6 In an interview with Siegel, Almodóvar comments that he was trying to make a kind of *How to Marry a Millionaire* 'with elegant, well-dressed women talking about men in a fantastic penthouse with artificial views of the town. No reality. If you work in this genre you can't include a blow-job or drugs. It violates the genre and the aesthetics. *Women on the Verge* is about 48 hours in the lives of several women. They are running around and so hysterical, they don't have time to have sex and take drugs. Sex, drugs, and all these fantastic and dirty things require time and then more time to recover' (1988: 88).

7 This scene is also discussed by Deletyo (1995: 52–3) and by Smith (1994: 96).

8 See also Nowell-Smith (1987) writing on melodramatic aesthetics.

9 See Charles Taylor's interview with Almodóvar in the *San Francisco Examiner*: 'I like them [i.e. melodramas] because they're not afraid of being ridiculous; they are so extreme. Other people would feel ashamed of saying what they say. In real life, people are so restrained, and melodrama is so daring in how it speaks about passion . . . I like the manifestation of passion with no shame' (1988). See also Murphy (1990: 33–40) and, on kitsch, Boyero (1981: 44).

10 Margaret Walters writes 'Clothes, I suspect are what the film is really about: the camera lovingly and fetishistically closes in on details – earrings, necklines, the sheen on Pepa's tights, most of all her high heels . . .' (1989: 3). David Hansen adds: 'Almodóvar's heroes are exuberant sinners, never saints. His world is painted with a bold and brazen palette: the deep purple of the 50s and 60s Hollywood melodramas he adores, the flaming red camp, the lurid blues of blue movies, the yellows of pop culture, and the pink champagne of boulevard farce. Conspicuously banished from his very urban movies are earth tones ...' (1988).

11 See Babington and Evans (1989: 1–44).

12 On Cifesa's reflection of dominant ideology, see Hopewell (1986).

13 In an interview (*El País*, 21 April 1995, pp. 14–15), Banderas has said that Don Juan is a role he would like to play.

14 The fluidity and versatility of Almodóvar's camera in this film should be noted. Almodóvar, in Lorenci (1988), explains: 'The tone of the film demanded it; it's a much more stylised film than the ones I had made previously, and undoubtedly the one that gave me most work to do. High, sophisticated crazy comedy doesn't give you any margin and if you're not on the ball it can all go wrong very easily.'

15 Though appearing in a small role in *Dark Habits*, Marisa Paredes has only recently taken on major roles in Almodóvar's films.

16 The play is a narrative of 'star-crossed' lovers whose trysts are arranged by the play's bawd, the eponymous Celestina.

Credits

**WOMEN ON THE
VERGE OF A NERVOUS
BREAKDOWN
(Mujeres al borde de un
ataque de nervios)**

Spain
1988

Director
Pedro Almodóvar

Production companies
Laurenfilm/El Deseo S.A.

Executive producer
Agustin Almodóvar

Associate producer
Antonio Lloréns

Production manager
Ester García

Unit managers
David Jareño, Daniel
Miranda

Assistant producer
Alejandro Vásquez

2nd assistant producers
Juan Carlos Caro, Carlos
Lázaro

Production assistant
Juan Carlos Garrido

Assistant directors
Julián Núñez, Miguel Angel
Pérez Campos

2nd assistant director
Tomás Corrales

Script supervisor
Marisa Ibarra

Casting
Nueva Agencia

Screenplay
Pedro Almodóvar

Photography
José Luis Alcaine

Camera operator
Alfredo Mayo

Assistant camera
Joaquin Manchado

2nd assistant camera
Juan Carlos Rodríguez

Key grip
Carlos Miguel

Gaffer
Fulcencio Rodríguez

Stills
Macusa Cores

Editor
José Salcedo

Assistant editors
Rosa Maria Ortiz, Manolo
Laguna

Special effects
Reyes Abades

Art director
Félix Murcia

Assistant art director
Carlos García Cambero

Set decorator
Federico del Cerro

Costume designer
José Maria de Cossío

Wardrobe
Peris Hnos, Cornejo

Hairstyles
Jesús Moncusi

Title design/graphics
Studio Gatti

Opticals
Pablo Núñez

Music
Bernardo Bonezzi

**Music recording
engineer**
Tino Azores

Additional music
'Soy infeliz' by Ventura
Rodgriguez, performed by
Lola Beltrán; 'Puro teatro'
by C. Curet Alonso,
performed by La Lupe;
'Spanish Caprice',
'Sheherezade' by Nikolai
Rimsky-Korsakov

Sound
Gilles Ortion

Mixing engineer
Eduardo Fernández

Sound effects
Luis Castro

Boom operator
Antonio Rodríguez

Animals
Francisco Ardura

89 Minutes
8011 feet

Carmen Maura
Pepa

Antonio Banderas
Carlos

Julieta Serrano
Lucía

María Barranco
Candela

Rossy de Palma
Marisa

Guillermo Montesinos
Taxi driver

Kiti Manver
Paulina

Chus Lampreave
Ivan's concierge

Yayo Calvo
Grandfather

Loles León
Christina

Angel de Andrés López
1st policeman

Fernando Guillén
Ivan

Juan Lombardero
Germán

José Antonio Navarro
2nd policeman

Ana Leza
Ana

Ambite
Ambite

Mary González
Mother Lucia

Lupe Parrado
Paulina's secretary

Joaquín Climent
Policeman, Spot I

Chema Gil
Policeman, Spot II

Gabriel Latorre
Priest

Francisco Caballero
TV newscaster

Carlos García Cambero
Repairman

Agustín Almodóvar
*Real estate agent
employee*

Tomás Corrales
Garbageman

Eva Gonzáles
Female dancer

Carmen Espada
Pharmacist

Susana Miraño
1st woman with facial mask

Paquita Fernández
*2nd woman with facial
mask*

**Frederico García
Cambero**
Pharmacy clerk

Gregorio Ross
Doctor

Paco Virseda
Messenger

Imanol Uribe
Husband

José Marco
Padrino

References

Almodóvar, Pedro. 1988. *The Pressbook for Women on the Verge of a Nervous Breakdown* (Madrid: El Deseo).

———— 1991. *Patty Diphusa y otros textos* (Barcelona: Anagrama).

Althusser, Louis. 1977 (1971). *Lenin and Philosophy and Other Essays,* translated by Ben Brewster (London: NLB).

Alvarez, Lily et al. 1977. *Diagnosis sobre el amor y el sexo* (Barcelona: Plaza y Janés).

Babington, Bruce and Peter William Evans. 1989. *Affairs to Remember: The Hollywood Comedy of the Sexes* (Manchester: Manchester University Press).

Boyero, Carlos. 1981. 'La moda Almodóvar', *Casablanca* no. 23, pp. 43–5.

Brunovska, Karnick and Henry Jenkins. 1995. 'Introduction: Golden Eras and Blind Spots – Genre, History and Comedy', in Brunovska and Jenkins (eds), *Classical Hollywood*

Comedy (London & New York: Routledge), pp. 1–13.

Castellano, Koro. 1995. 'Antonio Banderas conquista Hollywood', *El País Semanal*, 22 January, pp. 12–21.

Claesson, Bent H. 1980 (1978). *Información sexual para jóvenes* (Madrid: Lóguez Ediciones).

Cocteau, Jean. 1983 (1930). *La Voix humaine* (Paris: Editions Stock).

D'Lugo, Marvin. 1991. 'Almodóvar's City of Desire', *Quarterly Review of Film and Video* vol. 13 no. 4, pp. 47–65.

Doane, Mary Ann. 1988. *The Desire to Desire: The Woman's Film of the 1940s* (London: Macmillan).

Deleyto, Celestino. 1995. 'Postmodernism and Parody in Pedro Almodóvar's *Mujeres al borde de un ataque de nervios* (1988)', *Forum for Modern Language Studies* vol. 31 no. 1, pp. 49–63.

Dio Bleichmar, E. 1995. 'The Secret in the Constitution of Female

Sexuality: The Effects of the Adult's Sexual Look upon the Subjectivity of the Girl', *Journal of Clinical Psychoanalysis* vol. 4 no. 3, pp. 331–42.

Elsaesser, Thomas. 1987 (1972).'Tales of Sound and Fury: Observations on the Family Melodrama', in Christine Gledhill (ed.), *Home Is Where the Heart Is: Studies in Melodrama and the Woman's Film* (London: BFI).

Falcón, Lidia. 1992. *Mujer y poder político.* Madrid: Vindicación Feminista.

Fassbinder, Rainer Werner. 1972. 'Six Films by Douglas Sirk', in John Halliday et al. (eds), *Douglas Sirk* (Edinburgh: Edinburgh Film Festival).

Fernández, Gloria and Ana Oliva. 1995. *Antonio Banderas: Tan sólo un actor* (Manresa: Grata Lectuar).

Fernández Santos, A. 1990. *El País,* 23 January, p. 35.

Floyd, Nigel. 1991. 'The New Man from La Mancha', *The Guardian,* 15 December.

Forbes, Jill. 1989. 'Ivan the Terrible: *Women on the Verge of a Nervous Breakdown*', *Sight and Sound* vol. 58 no. 2, p. 135.

Foucault, M. 1991 (1984). 'The Body of the Condemned', in Paul Rabinow, (ed.), *The Foucault Reader: An Introduction to Foucault's Thought* (Harmondsworth: Penguin) pp. 170–78.

Freud, Sigmund. 1981 (1912). 'On the Universal Tendency to Debasement in the Sphere of Love', in *The Penguin Freud Library: Vol. 7. On Sexuality* (Harmondsworth: Penguin), pp. 243–60.

García de León, María Antonia and Teresa Maldonado. 1989. *Pedro Almodóvar: La otra España cañí* (Ciudad Real: Diputación de Ciudad Real).

Gledhill, Christine, (ed.) 1991. *Stardom: Industry of Desire* (London and New York: Routledge).

Goñi, Miguel J. (ed.) 1980. *Enciclopedia práctica de la madre; 'la sexualidad'* (Madrid: Ediciones Nueva Lente).

Gual, R. Jordi. 1982. *Elementos de sexología para adolescentes* (Barcelona: Ediciones Cedel).

Gubern, Román. 1980. *La censura. Función política y ordenamiento jurídico bajo el franquismo (1939–1975)* (Barcelona: Ediciones Península).

Hansen, David. 1988. 'The Man of La Mancha: A Taboo-Smashing Director Revels in the New Spain', *Newsweek,* 5 December, p. 88.

Hopewell, John. 1986. *Out of the Past: Spanish Cinema after Franco* (London: BFI).

Horn, Richard. 1993. *Fifties Style* (New York: Friedman-Fairfax).

Horney, Karen. 1967. *Feminine Psychology,* ed. with an introduction by Harold Kelman (London: Routledge and Kegan Paul).

Instituto de Cinematografía y de las Artes Audiovisuales, Ministerio de Cultura de España. 1995. 'Las pelas de las pelis', *El País*, 22 December, pp. 18–19 [Information valid until 1994].

Kael, Pauline. 1988. 'The Current Cinema: Red on Red', *The New Yorker*, 16 May, pp. 96–7.

Kinder, Marsha. 1983. 'The Children of Franco in the New Spanish Cinema', *Quarterly Review of Film Studies* vol. 8 no. 2, Spring, pp. 57–76.

————— 1987. 'Pleasure and the New Spanish Mentality: Interview with Pedro Almodóvar', *Film Quarterly* no. 41, Autumn, pp. 33–43.

————— 1993. *Blood Cinema: The Reconstruction of National Identity in Spain* (Los Angeles: University of California Press).

Klein, Melanie and Joan Riviere. 1964. *Love, Hate and Reparation* (London and New York: Verso).

Lorenci, Miguel. 13.3.1988. '*Mujeres al borde de un ataque de nervios* la más madura y mejor película de Almodóvar', *Diario de Cádiz*.

Moix, Terenci. 1990. *El peso de la paja.* (Barcelona: Plaza y Janés).

Molina-Foix, Vicente. 1993. 'El hombre de mundo', *Cambio 16*, 27 September, p. 21.

Mulvey, Laura. 1975. 'Visual Pleasure and Narrative Cinema', *Screen* vol. 16 no. 3, Autumn, pp. 6–18.

Murphy, Ryan. 1990. 'Gay Director Pedro Almodóvar Refuses to Be Tied by Censorship', *The Advocate*, 19 June, pp. 33–40.

Nowell-Smith, Geoffrey. 1987. 'Minnelli and Melodrama', in Christine Gledhill (ed.), *Home Is Where the Heart Is: Studies in Melodrama and the Woman's Film* (London: BFI).

O'Toole, Lawrence. 1988. 'Almodóvar in Bondage', *Sight and Sound* vol. 59 no. 4, pp. 270–73.

Parker, Dorothy. 1989. *The Collected Dorothy Parker,* ed. Brendan Gill (Harmondsworth: Penguin Books).

Ponga, Paula. 1993. *Carmen Maura* (Barcelona: Mitografías).

Riviere, Joan. 1966. 'Womanliness as Masquerade', in Hendrick M. Ruitenbeck (ed.), *Psychoanalysis and Female Sexuality* (New Haven: College and UP).

Rowe, Kathleen. 1995. 'Comedy, Melodrama and Gender: Theorizing the Genre of Laughter' in Karnick Brunovska and Henry Jenkins (eds), *Classical Hollywood Comedy* (London & New York: Routledge).

Sánchez Ochoa, Pilar et al. 1992. *Mujer andaluza. ¿La caída de un mito?* (Brenes, Sevilla: Editorial Muñoz Moya y Montraveta).

Secunda, Victoria. 1993. *Women and Their Fathers: The Sexual and Romantic Impact of the First Man in Your Life* (London: Cedar).

Siegel, Joel E. 1988. 'A Talk with Pedro Almodóvar: Spanish Gadfly', *Washington Post,* 29 April, p. 88.

Smith, Paul Julian. 1994. *Desire Unlimited: The Cinema of Pedro Almodóvar* (London and New York: Verso).

Strauss, Frédéric. 1995. *Pedro Almodóvar: Un cine visceral. Conversaciones con Frédéric Strauss* (Madrid: El País Aguilar).

Taylor, Charles. 1988. 'Spanish Director Way of Success', *San Francisco Examiner*, 23 December.

Torres, Maruja. 1995. 'Pedro Almodóvar', *El País Semanal*, 17 September, pp. 36–42.

Triana Toribio, Nuria. 1993. *Subculture and Popular Culture in the Films of Pedro Almodóvar* (unpublished PhD., Newcastle University).

Villaverde, Daniel. 1988. 'Almodóvar: Las mujeres lloran mejor', *La Nueva España,* 26 March.

Vincendeau, Ginette (ed.), 1995. *Encyclopaedia of European Film* (London: BFI).

Walters, Margaret. 1989. 'Kitsch and Make-Up', *The Listener*, 15 June, p. 3.

BFI Modern Classics is an exciting new series
which combines careful research with high quality
writing about contemporary cinema. Authors write
on a film of their choice, making the case for its
elevation to the status of classic. The series will
grow into an influential and authoritative commentary
on all that is best in the cinema of our time.
If you would like to receive further information about
future **BFI Modern Classics** or about other books on
film, media and popular culture from BFI Publishing,
please fill in your name and address and return this
card to the BFI*.
No stamp needed if posted in the UK, Channel
Islands, or Isle of Man.

NAME

_____

_____

ADDRESS

_____

_____

POSTCODE

_____

* North America: Please return your card to:
Indiana University Press, Attn: LPB, 601 N Morton Street,
Bloomington, IN 47401-3797

BFI Publishing
21 Stephen Street
FREEPOST 7
LONDON
W1E 4AN